THE SENIOR SOLUTION

A Family Guide to Keeping Seniors Home for Life!

Valerie VanBooven–Whitsell RN, BSN, PGCM

LTC Expert Publications, LLC
St. Louis, MO

The Senior Solution:
A Family Guide to Keeping Seniors Home for Life!

Copyright © 2007 by Valerie VanBooven-Whitsell and Next Generation Financial Services. Printed and bound in the United States of America. All rights reserved. No part of this book may be reproduced or transmitted in any form or by any means, electronic or mechanical, including photocopying, recording, or by any information storage and retrieval system—except by a reviewer who may quote brief passages in a review to be printed in a magazine, newspaper, or on the Web—without permission in writing from the publisher. For information, please contact LTC Expert Publications, LLC, at 877-529-0550 or on the web at *www.theltcexpert.com*.

Although the author and publisher have made every effort to ensure the accuracy and completeness of information contained in this book, we assume no responsibility for errors, inaccuracies, omissions, or any inconsistency herein. Any slights of people, places, or organizations are unintentional.

First printing 2007

Published by:
LTC EXPERT PUBLICATIONS, LLC
St. Louis, MO
877-529-0550
Email: Valerie@theltcexpert.com
Web: www.theltcexpert.com
ISBN: 978-0-9743373-3-3
LCCN: 2007902960

ATTENTION CORPORATIONS, UNIVERSITIES, COLLEGES, AND PROFESSIONAL ORGANIZATIONS: Quantity discounts are available on bulk purchases of this book for educational, gift purposes, or as premiums for increasing magazine subscriptions or renewals. Special books or book excerpts can also be created to fit specific needs. For information, please contact LTC Expert Publications, at 877-529-0550, or on the web at *www.theltcexpert.com*.

Cover Design and Interior Design © TLC Graphics, *www.TLCGraphics.com*
Edited by JoAnne Lorensen, M.Ed.
Printed and bound by Bang Printing, Brainerd, Minnesota

Contributing Authors:
Troy Shellhammer
Althea West, MA Gerontology
Gene Pastula, CFP

Dedication

This book is dedicated to adult children of aging parents, caregivers, seniors, and people who are tireless advocates of the elderly, and quality long-term care. There are those of you who no longer have a voice—I am proud to have served as your advocate and your protector in a time of need. For those of you who still have a voice, keep expressing, keep advocating, and keep reaching out and educating others. From you, I learn something new everyday. To my family, friends, and loved ones, thank you for your patience, your support, your encouragement, and your influence. I do believe that anything is possible. To all of my colleagues at Next Generation Financial Services, thank you for *knowing* that there are better ways to serve seniors, and that there are tools and resources that make seniors' lives better. To my husband Charles Lee Whitsell and my children, the triplets—Madeline Anne Whitsell, Sophia Belle Whitsell, and Samantha Lee Whitsell, born March 5, 2007. Thank you for everything, you make life wonderful!

Table of Contents

Introduction xi
    The Message xii

Part I: Seniors Facing Crisis 1

Senior Solution #1:
The Elephant Standing In The Room
Needs To Be Addressed Quickly 3
    Who is Going to Take Care of Mom and Dad? 5
    How Long Can Seniors Be Cared for
        at Home—Realistically? 6
    How Can We Keep Seniors Safe in Their Own Homes? 7
    Personal Emergency Response Systems 8

Senior Solution #2:
Managing Long-Term Care Includes Having
Legal Documentation in Order. 11
    Legal Matters 11
    What is a "Power of Attorney"? 11

Advanced Directives (Living Wills) 13
Revocable Living Trust. 14
Irrevocable Trusts—Be Careful! 15

Senior Solution #3:
Understand That Medicare
Does NOT Pay For Long-Term Care. 17

"I'm Already Covered, Right?" 17
Medicare and Other Health Insurances 17
What Will Medicare Pay? 18
What Will Medicare A and B NOT Pay For? 18
Medicare Supplements. 19
Medicare HMOs 20
Private Insurance 20
Disability Insurance 20
Veteran's Administration Benefits. 20
VA Home Aid and Attendant Services Grant. 21

Senior Solution #4:
Understand What Applying for Medicaid
Really Means—Before You Apply 23

Medicaid Defined 23
Deficit Reduction Act 2005. 24
Changes to Medicaid Eligibility. 24
Reverse Mortgages and Medicaid. 26
Prenuptial Agreements. 27
Mandatory Estate Recovery 28
Transferring Assets 28

TABLE OF CONTENTS

Senior Solution #5:
Using a Reverse Mortgage to Keep Mom and Dad at Home Longer Might Be the Best Option........ 31

What is a (HECM) Reverse Mortgage?..................... 33

Who Qualifies for a Reverse Mortgage?.................... 33

How Are Seniors Protected?............................. 33

How Can the Cash Flow From a Reverse Mortgage
Keep Mom and Dad at Home Longer? 34

Does the Senior's Name Remain
on The Title to the Home?............................. 34

Can Their Home Be Taken Away from Them? 34

Will Heirs Be Responsible for Repaying This Loan? 34

When Does the Loan Come Due?....................... 35

Can Mom and Dad Still Leave
Their Home to Their Children? 35

How Does the Deficit Reduction
Act 2005 Affect Home Equity?......................... 35

Senior Solution #6:
Surrounding Yourself/Your Family With a Team of Experts is the Best Medicine 39

Financial Advisors Helping Seniors
with Cash Flow Planning.............................. 39

Finding a Trusted Advisor Who Can Help................. 39

Elder Law Attorneys 40

Geriatric Care Management as a Resource................. 40

Recommendations for Choosing
a Geriatric Care Manager............................. 42

My Parent Doesn't Want Any Help,
What Should I Do?.................................. 43

Senior Solution #7:
Attention Adult Children and Family Members Caring for an Aging Adult—Give Yourself a Break.........45

When the Caregiver Needs a Break…
Where Can They Turn? 45

Hospice Care—At the End of Life...................... 47

Pay Yourself or a Loved One for
Providing Care—The Options and Tax Benefits........... 48

Tax Deductions and Benefits for Caregivers................ 49

Talk to Employers About Dependent Care FSAs............ 51

Senior Solution #8:
Living at Home is Possible, and A Lot Easier When You Know What Questions to Ask 53

Tips and Hints for Choosing an In-Home Care Service 53

Medical vs. Non-Medical In-Home Care Services 54

Adult Day Care 55

Transportation Resources for Seniors....................... 57

Senior Solution #9:
Alternative Living Arrangements Can Be a Positive Experience 61

Continuum Of Care Retirement Communities (CCRC)...... 62

Assisted Living Facilities................................. 62

Nursing Home Care 63

Tips for Choosing an Assisted Living
or Nursing Care Facility............................... 63

TABLE OF CONTENTS

Part 2: Planning Ahead for Long-Term Care—Avoid The Crisis! 65

Senior Solution #1:
Planning Ahead for Long-Term Care Means Evaluating All of the Options. 67

How Much Does Long-Term Care Insurance Cost?. 67

Affording Long-Term Care Insurance Without Touching a Penny of Your Savings, Investments, or Current Income. 67

Traditional Long-Term Care Insurance 69

Who CAN'T Get Long-Term Care Insurance? 69

Qualifying to USE Your Long-Term Care Insurance 70

Comprehensive vs. Facility Only Plans 70

Important Considerations When Choosing a Long-Term Care Insurance Plan. 77

Tax Considerations 78

Tax Qualified Plans vs. Non-Tax Qualified Plans. 79

Payment Options for Long-Term Care Insurance 79

The Pension Protection Act of 2006 81

Asset Based Long-Term Care Insurance. 81

Life Settlements. 84

Senior Solution #2:
The Best New Way to Consider Your Estate Planning Needs— Using Home Equity to Your Advantage 89

Passing on the Value of Your Home to Your Heirs. 89

Conclusion. 93

The Senior Solution Rolodex 95
Financial Planning Assistance. 95
Reverse Mortgage Information and Services. 96
Life Settlements 96
Long-Term Care Insurance/Health Insurance 97
Government Agencies of Interest 98
Legal Resources 100
Caregiver Resources: Home Care and Adult Day Care 100
Caregiver Resources: Hospice. 101
Caregiver Resources: Housing 102
Caregiver Resources: Geriatric Care Management 103
Caregiver Resources: Medications 103
Caregiver Resources: Finding Doctors 104
Caregiver Resources: Caregiver Organizations
    and Support 104
Other Caregiver Sites of Interest 105
Senior Advocacy and Interest Groups 105
Miscellaneous Sites of Interest 107
Specific Disease, Medical Conditions
    and Organizations On-Line 107

About the Author 109

Introduction

We have lived with the myths of long-term care long enough. We believe that it will never happen to us, our current health insurance plan will pay for long-term care, and that planning ahead is too expensive and difficult. The reality is: chances are we *will* need long-term care, our current health insurance was *never* designed to pay for it, and *not* planning ahead is more expensive and difficult than taking a proactive approach.

Today there are many tools and resources that keep seniors "home for life". Long-term care insurance, reverse mortgages, VA home aid and attendant pension benefits, and personal emergency response systems are just a *few* of the many options that exist for seniors and their family members. Knowing how to access this information is the first step toward avoiding crisis.

Most of us would like to live a long, healthy life. But with a long healthy life comes a series of decisions and possible complications that need to be addressed before it's too late. Long-term care is not a topic that is easily discussed on Sunday afternoon, with the family gathered around the kitchen table. In fact, discussing long-term care and planning ahead for long-term care has been, and continues to be, one of America's least favorite things to do.

The intention of this book is to help families start that conversation and unravel the myths of long-term care. It doesn't matter whether you are a 30-something, a baby-boomer, or a 70-something…long-term care is a family matter. It affects all of us. It affects our personal lives and our careers. We may be the 30-something faced with caring for an aging parent or we may be a baby-boomer trying to decide the best way to plan ahead. For anyone who has been approached about the need for long-term care insurance and for anyone who has had a long-term care "experience" in their family, this book was designed to turn myth into reality, and provide useful common-sense information from a healthcare professional who has worked in all aspects of the long-term care continuum.

It is important to understand that increased longevity, changes in family structure, changes in the workplace, changes in medical care, and the insurance industry in general, all have contributed to the need for pre-planning. Planning ahead for long-term care requires a proactive approach and a positive attitude.

- People who plan ahead, do so for various reasons including:
- To protect and preserve assets for themselves and their children.
- Wanting to maintain independence and choice.
- Wanting to receive quality care.
- Not wanting to be a burden to their family members.
- Not wanting to end up impoverished and on Medicaid.

For others the situation is a bit different. Long-term care is already happening, or HAS happened. There was no time to plan ahead or it just wasn't done. Therefore, family members are faced with trying to provide the best care in the best circumstances possible.

The Message

The message is clear. Understanding the secrets to long-term care planning, caregiving, and crisis management is essential for all families who want to keep their seniors home for life. Planning ahead for long-term care has never been more important.

INTRODUCTION

We are on the verge of an exploding aging population. According to the U.S Census Bureau, *7,918 boomers will turn 60 each day in 2006.* (Not to suggest that anyone should wait until they are age 60 to plan for later years.) Of the 78.2 million boomers July 1, 2005, a slim majority—50.8%—were women. In 25 years, however, their majority margin will be almost 10%; 57.8 million boomers are expected to be still alive, and 54.8% will be women.

The Medicaid system is a disaster. It is imperative to understand that long-term care is not a matter of entitlement. Long-term care *is* the responsibility of each individual. How we plan ahead, how we pay for it, and how and where we are cared for, is up to each one of us.

Families who are now faced with caring for an aging parent or relative, need resources and information that will assist them in making the best decisions possible regarding care. If your parent or aging loved one is in need of services, or is currently in a long-term care crisis, there is hope. Educating ourselves about services that are currently available is imperative and makes the journey much easier for the entire family.

Hear the message before it is too late. Do something rather than nothing at all. Not making a decision is a decision in itself. Be an informed consumer and make a choice that will not only affect you personally, but will allow your family members the opportunity for peace of mind down the road.

It is important for all of us to understand and use the tools available to us to maintain autonomy, dignity and independence in our later years. It's just a matter of understanding the concepts! This book, "The Senior Solution" helps families and seniors understand how to manage long-term care crisis points in life, and plan ahead to avoid a long-term care crisis, using all of the options available to us today.

PART ONE

Seniors Facing Crisis

SENIOR SOLUTION #1

The Elephant Standing In The Room Needs To Be Addressed Quickly

---

The biggest and most obvious elephant standing in the room for seniors and for long-term care needs is usually *money*. How in the *world* are we going to pay for long-term care?

The Cost of Care Looks Like This:

- The national average daily rate for a private room in a nursing home is **$206, or $75,190** annually.

- The national average daily rate for a semi-private room in a nursing home is **$183, or $66,795** annually.

- The national average hourly rate for home health aides is **$19**. For only 5 hours of care 7 days per week, the monthly average cost is **$2660 per month or $31,920** annually.

- The national average hourly rate for homemakers/companions is **$17**. For only 5 hours of care 7 days per week, the monthly average cost is **$2380 per month or $28,560** annually.

Privately paying for long-term care means that seniors would have to find an additional $28,560 to $75,190 per year in their budget for just

ONE person to receive care. Most of us, seniors or not, could not afford to privately pay for our own care year after year.

Long-term care insurance will pay for in-home care, assisted living, and nursing home care. This is the most appropriate and needed form of insurance protection available to us today. Long-term care insurance should be termed "lifestyle" insurance (it's NOT nursing home insurance!). If your vision of your later years includes sitting at home in your own recliner, with your own remote control, watching your own TV....well, you should be planning for that future with long-term care insurance. In later chapters we discuss all of the options related to long-term care insurance today.

Reverse mortgages (Home Equity Conversion Mortgages) have become one of the most popular and accepted way of paying for many different expenses, including the cost of long-term care. Reverse mortgages are designed to keep seniors at home longer. A reverse mortgage can pay for in-home care, home repair, home modification, and any other need a senior may have. Almost every chapter moving forward in this book discusses the use of reverse mortgages for seniors in some way. That's how important this cash flow planning concept has become in recent years.

Government assistance should be a last resort when considering how to pay for long-term care. This type of assistance refers to relying on the Medicaid system. Medicaid will pay for long-term care for seniors who cannot afford to pay for care themselves. Keep in mind that Medicaid is an under-funded and over-burdened system, therefore Medicaid resources are limited. This means that in many areas Medicaid beds in nursing homes are difficult to find. Families may end up driving long distances to visit their loved ones. Traditionally, Medicaid resources for in-home care are extremely limited, which means most seniors who apply for Medicaid end up in a nursing home type setting. The Deficit Reduction Act 2005 makes qualifying for Medicaid even more difficult for most families. An in depth discussion of Medicaid appears later in the book. Planning ahead is really the only viable option for families today.

SENIOR SOLUTION #1

Who is Going to Take Care of Mom and Dad?

According to a recent joint Cornell and Purdue University study, supported by the National Institute on Aging, aging mothers are nearly four times more likely to expect a daughter to assume the role of their caregiver rather than a son if they become ill or disabled.

These mothers also are much more likely to choose a child to whom they feel emotionally close and who has values similar to their own, report Karl Pillemer, Professor of Human Development at Cornell, and Purdue sociologist Jill Suitor, in the journal, "The Gerontologist". (*The Gerontologist* 46:439-448 (2006) © 2006 *The Gerontological Society of America* Making Choices: A Within-Family Study of Caregiver Selection **Karl Pillemer, PhD**[1,] **and J. Jill Suitor, PhD**[2])

Aging adults today who are on the threshold of needing additional assistance in the home are also aging adults who tended to have larger families during their childbearing years. It is important, although admittedly often difficult for seniors to talk with their adult children about expectations and wishes. It's also important for adult children to talk with each other about who will be assuming what role with regard to helping Mom and Dad. No discussion at all can lead to disappointment, confusion and disagreement between siblings.

Long-term care is a family issue, but it is more often a woman's issue. Throughout history women have been the caregivers in our lives. As we have seen, women also live longer than men on average. From beginning to end, women often care for family members young and old. Now as our population begins to age, it is even more important that we understand what lies before us.

Although we see increases in male caregivers all the time, the fact remains, that when it comes to long-term care for our family members and our spouses, today women carry the weight.

Daughters, daughters-in-law, wives, sisters and nieces often accept the role of caregiver for aging adults in the family. Across the U.S. there are women commonly referred to as "the sandwich generation" who are playing dual roles in their families. They are often mothers themselves, while caring for their own aging parents at the same time. The level of stress and frustration can be overwhelming. Careers are being put on hold, and promotions passed up, in order to accommodate the busy schedules of their children, and their parents. Even so, there is still not enough time for these women to meet everyone's needs. A financial burden results as well.

Women in America also tend to marry men who are older than they are. Therefore, they often end up caring for a chronically ill spouse in later years. When this happens, it is sometimes the case that all of the retirement funding and assets are used to pay for the long-term care needs of the "ill" spouse, leaving nothing in savings to care for the "well" spouse later in life.

It is estimated that one out of two women will need long-term care at some point in their lives. One out of three men will also require long-term care. So why do more women need services? A woman's life expectancy is still longer than the average male.

> Tip: If for any reason a senior couple CAN get long-term care insurance for **just one spouse**, DO IT! If the male spouse gets sick first, and assets are used to pay for his care, the female spouse will still have means to pay for her own long-term care through insurance. Don't disregard long-term care insurance just because **one** of you can't qualify for it due to health, or it's not affordable for both. Cover at least one spouse whenever possible!

How Long Can Seniors Be Cared for at Home—Realistically?

The answer to this question depends on many things, but ultimately it depends on how much support seniors have in their own community from family, friends, neighbors, religious organizations, and ease of access to the medical system. Cash flow, as previously discussed, is another factor that determines how long seniors can stay at home safely.

Set up properly, a senior can stay in his or her own home for their entire life. As long as care can be paid for, or provided by family members locally, and as long as the living situation is safe and comfortable, seniors stay at home. In the next few chapters we will give you more information on how this can be achieved.

It is important to note that according to a study by the National Association of Home Builders 50+ Housing Council, for those owning single family homes, 35.9% of households in the 55 to 64 age group reported difficulty in at least one physical activity:

- difficulty in dressing (9%);
- vision or hearing difficulty (11%);
- difficulty in going out (11.9%);
- difficulty in walking, reaching, lifting, carrying, climbing stairs or getting around the house (27.1%);
- difficulty in remembering (12.7%);
- and difficulty in working (23.8%).
- More than 45% of those 65 to 74 and 70% of households 75 or older reported difficulty in some activity.

(March 2007, National Association of Home Builders 50+ Housing Council Study- Aging Boomers May Be Hard to Budge From Current Homes)

How Can We Keep Seniors Safe in Their Own Homes?

Keeping seniors safe includes making sure that the interior and exterior of the home is up-to-code, senior friendly, and accessible for those who are disabled. Interior safety includes modifications such as safety grab bars in the bathrooms, elevated toilet seats and lower sink and vanity heights if needed. Kitchen cabinets can be lowered for easier accessibility. Doorways in older homes may be too narrow for walkers and wheelchairs, and may need to be widened if possible. Levered door handles are a plus for everyone. Throw rugs are a bad idea in a senior's home. They contribute to falls more often than not. On the exterior of the home there should be sturdy handrails wherever there are steps or uneven pavement. Senior friendly homes are now constructed on one level with no steps at the front door or garage entry. Many home builders are now specialized in senior living and are available for consultation.

Personal Emergency Response Systems

Personal emergency response systems (PERS) are another form of safety that should always be addressed. A "PERS" is a system that can be set up very inexpensively in a senior's home. This isn't just for "sick" people. These systems keep well people well. The senior wears a pendant around their neck, or a watch style pendant, and has the system with them at all times inside and outside of the house. If they suffer a fall, stroke, illness, or any other event where they feel they might need assistance, all they have to do is access their system with the touch of a button.

Statistics:

A study by AC Nielson indicates among other things that seniors who have a personal emergency response system *stay at home an average of 6 years longer* than those who do not have a PERS. Also most PERS have smoke detector options, keeping the home safe and protected from fire devastation.

- 58% of customers with a PERS for a year or more feel that their quality of life has improved.
- 87% of customers with a PERS think that this protection is important or a main factor in their decision to continue living at home.
- 95% of customer with a PERS feel protected at home.
- 80% feel that the comfort of living in their own home is important.
- 76% feel that being independent is important.

SENIOR SOLUTION #1

> In a study of older adults, those living with a PERS reported significantly greater ability to go about daily routine and were **ten times** less likely to require admission to a nursing home.

Medical research shows that falling down and being unable to get help is not an uncommon event. In fact, nearly *1/3* of all people over the age of 65 (and *half* of all people over 90) will fall each year. Of course the older a senior gets, the more dangerous and debilitating falls can be, and they often mark the end of independent living.

Research also tells us that 30% to 50% of elderly people fear falling—a fear that can cause them to lose confidence and restrict their normal range of healthy activities. The confidence and peace-of-mind that comes from a PERS helps to ease these anxieties, as well as the feelings of isolation and depression caused by such worries.

Facts About Personal Emergency Response Systems

- **PERS are recommended by doctors, nurses and other professional caregivers.** They know even a minor fall or incident can have serious physical and psychological consequences if a senior can't get help in a hurry.

- **A PERS is for independent living at home.** The alternative to getting a PERS is often assisted living, a nursing home, or 24-hour care.

- **A PERS is a good idea even if a senior doesn't live alone.** Accidents are unpredictable. A senior might need help when someone they live with is temporarily out of the house.

- **A PERS is easy to live with.** The personal help button is very small, simple to use and won't interfere with a senior's activities in any way.

- **A PERS is for everyday living.** A PERS telephone also includes many other features that makes conversing with others more convenient and can provide personalized reminders of important things to do.

The Stephenson Family Story

Jim and Sue Stephenson (ages 72 and 65) have lived in the same home in Des Moines, IA for 30 years. Admittedly, their home is less than senior friendly. Jim's knee problems make it difficult for him to get up and down the stairs. He and his family know that he is at a significant risk for falling. Their 2-story home is worth about $150,000 and is paid in full. They do not want to move at this time. Jim and Sue's children have become increasingly worried about the two of them living at home without assistance. After a one-hour consultation and some education on the options, the Stephenson's decided to take action. Home modification and repair were one of their first priorities, but the repairs would be expensive. Jim and Sue decided to take out a reverse mortgage to help them afford the needed maintenance. They were able to receive approximately $71,000 from the equity in their home. They used the cash to install a stair lift for Jim ($2500). They also installed safety bars in all bathrooms and showers and installed a safety rail in the hallway for Jim to hold on to if needed ($800). They then decided to purchase a personal emergency response system for their home in the event that Jim or Sue need additional assistance ($35/month). Sue and her children could feel comfortable leaving Jim at home for short periods of time—long enough to do the grocery shopping or run other errands. Jim and Sue's children have peace of mind knowing that their parents are safe. Jim and Sue left the rest of the money from the reverse mortgage in a "line of credit" and will access it as needed for further repairs, maintenance or upgrades.

SENIOR SOLUTION #2

Managing Long-Term Care Includes Having Legal Documentation in Order

Legal Matters

One of the most important things to set in motion is taking care of the legal paperwork! A Durable Power of Attorney for Health Care and a Financial Power of Attorney are essential, along with an Advanced Directive or Living Will.

What is a "Power of Attorney"?

Power of Attorney (POA) is a document whereby one person (called the "principal") authorizes another individual or entity (called an "agent" or "attorney-in-fact") to act on behalf of the principal. The most common uses for a POA are financial transactions and health care decisions. Most states have one set of laws governing financial POAs and second set of laws governing POAs for health care decisions. Therefore, it is the common and recommended practice not to mix the two purposes into one document. An individual desiring to have a POA covering both financial and medical situations should prepare two separate POAs, one dealing with financial issues and the second dealing with medical issues.

When Should I Have a Financial Power of Attorney?

Persons with physical handicaps or limitations often set up financial POAs, with a family member as the agent, to allow the family member to do such routine matters as making withdrawals from the principal's bank account. It would otherwise be a burden for the principal with physical limitations to make the short trips personally to perform the banking transactions.

The second reason for preparation of a financial POA is preventative in nature. If you lose the mental capacity to handle your own financial affairs, without a durable power of attorney (see below), your family members will need to go to court and have a guardian or conservator appointed over your assets. If you have previously set up a durable power of attorney and then lose mental capacity, the agent named in your POA will be able to handle your financial affairs without the time and attorney fees necessary of going to the court to get a guardian and conservator appointed.

A "Durable" POA is one that remains in force even after the principal (i.e., the individual who executed the POA) loses mental capacity. Unless a POA is "durable", it will become ineffective at the time the principal becomes incompetent. Thus, a POA which is not "durable" fails to protect you against the potential of your family having to go to court and get a guardian and conservator appointed over your assets.

What Makes a Power of Attorney "Durable"?

This is a matter of state law. The Uniform Durable Power of Attorney Act has been adopted by 48 states and provides the following definition:

> "A durable power of attorney is a power of attorney by which a principal, in writing, designates another as his attorney in fact and the writing contains the words, 'This power of attorney shall not be affected by subsequent disability or incapacity of the principal', or 'This power of attorney shall become effective upon the disability or incapacity of the principal', or similar words showing the intent of the principal that the authority conferred shall

continue notwithstanding the subsequent disability or incapacity of the principal."

Therefore, the first requirement is that there be a written and signed document and second, the document contains words such as those above which clearly indicate that the principal intended the POA to be effective even after he or she became incapacitated. Although the language of the Uniform Act does not specifically state whether the document must also be notarized in order to be durable, the form recommended by the uniform laws commission has a space for the signature of a notary. Most states require POAs to be notarized to be durable and for them to be effective for real estate transactions. It is recommended that your POA be notarized. Also, some states require witnesses to the principal's signature.

Advanced Directives (Living Wills)

Any healthcare professional will tell you that having an Advanced Directive (Living Will) may be the most important document you ever put together in your entire life. Having an advanced directive helps adult children, or any loved one, understand your wishes for the end of your life when you are no able longer to communicate those wishes yourself.

The term "advanced directive" refers to legal means by which individuals can express and, within certain limits, enforce their wishes regarding health care in the event that they become unconscious or otherwise mentally incapacitated. Common examples include living wills (which may direct families and physicians to withhold or withdraw life support if the person is terminally ill and permanently unconscious) and durable powers of attorney (which appoint and invest third parties with full authority to make decisions regarding healthcare for incapacitated patients). When properly set up, these documents provide those who, in good faith, follow their provisions with protection from prosecution and civil suit.

A good elder law attorney (*www.naela.org*) can assist you and your family members draft an advanced directive, and most hospitals today will provide the forms and notaries for you upon admission to the hospital.

Five Wishes

One example of an advanced directive is called "Five Wishes". The Five Wishes document helps you express how you want to be treated if you are seriously ill and unable to speak for yourself. It is unique among all other living will and health agent forms because it looks to all of a person's needs: medical, personal, emotional and spiritual. Five Wishes also encourages discussing your wishes with your family and physician. Additional information can be found at *www.agingwithdignity.org*

Five Wishes Lets Your Family and Doctors Know:

- Which person you want to make health care decisions for you when you can't make them.
- The kind of medical treatment you want or don't want.
- How comfortable you want to be.
- How you want people to treat you.
- What you want your loved ones to know.

Revocable Living Trust

This is a trust created by an individual (the trustor), and administered by another party (the trustee), while the trustor is still alive. The individual creating the living trust can be his or her own trustee while they are living and not incapacitated. Upon the individual's death, a successor trustee named in the trust will become the administrator. A living trust can be either revocable or irrevocable. At the time of death, a living trust avoids probate in court and therefore gets assets of the estate distributed much more quickly and with less cost than a will does. It also offers a higher level of confidentiality, as probate proceedings are a matter of public record. Additionally, trusts are usually harder to contest than wills.

On the downside, a living trust takes longer to put together than a will, and requires more ongoing maintenance. Although both a will and a living trust can be modified or revoked at any time before death, such changes are slightly more time-consuming for a living trust. Additionally, assets that a person wants to move to a living trust, such as real estate and bank or brokerage accounts, have to be re-titled in the name of the trust.

Irrevocable Trusts—Be Careful!

An *irrevocable trust* is an arrangement in which the grantor departs with ownership and control of property. Usually this involves a gift of the property to the trust. The trust then stands as a separate taxable entity and pays tax on its accumulated income. Trusts typically receive a deduction for income that is distributed on a current basis. Because the grantor must permanently depart with the ownership and control of the property being transferred to an irrevocable trust, such a device has limited appeal to most taxpayers.

Homes that have put into an irrevocable trust are generally not eligible for a reverse mortgage. An irrevocable living trust is typically used in very advanced estate planning strategies.

SENIOR SOLUTION #3

Understand that Medicare Does NOT Pay for Long-Term Care

"I'm Already Covered, Right?"

There is a common misconception that health insurance will pay for the cost of long-term care. Health insurance including Medicare, Medicare Supplements, HMOs, private insurance through employers, and disability insurance were never designed to pay for the cost of long-term care.

Medicare and Other Health Insurances

Medicare is a federal health insurance program for people 65 and older, certain people with disabilities, and ESRD (End Stage Renal Disease). It pays for much of your health care, but not all of it. There are some costs you will have to pay yourself. (*www.medicare.gov*)

There are other kinds of health insurance that may help pay the costs that Medicare does not. Medicare Supplements (Medigap Policies) and Long-Term Care Insurance will pick up some of the costs that Medicare will not pay for.

Medicare was implemented in 1965. How many times has Medicare been over-hauled since 1965? NEVER. It was not designed to pay for care related to diseases or conditions such as Alzheimer's disease, Parkinson's, or MS. The average life expectancy was much lower in 1965 because medical technology was not as advanced. Medicare was designed for SHORT-TERM acute care, and short-term rehabilitative stays in a rehab or long-term care facility. Although Medicare Part D was added in 2004/2005 to help with the costs of prescription drugs, Medicare still does not pay for long-term care.

What Will Medicare Pay?

Medicare comes in three parts. Medicare Part A and Part B, and now Part D for prescription drugs.

Medicare Part A is Hospital Insurance

Part A pays for inpatient hospital care, some skilled nursing facility care, hospice care, and some home health care. Most people get Medicare Part A automatically when they turn 65. There is usually no premium or monthly payment for Part A.

Medicare Part B is Medical Insurance

Part B pays for doctor's services, outpatient hospital care, and some other medical services that Part A doesn't pay for. Part B pays for these services and supplies when they are medically necessary. Part B has a premium that changes every year.

What Will Medicare A and B NOT Pay For?

Medicare carries some high deductibles. For instance in 2007, during a hospital stay you will automatically have a $992 total deductible for days 1-60. On day 61 you are responsible for $248 (your deductible) per day through day 90. On day 91 you pay $496 per day (your deductible) through day 150. This amounts to a substantial out-of-pocket expense for the Medicare recipient.

For a skilled nursing facility stay, Medicare pays for days 1-20. On day 21 you pay $124.00 per day deductible through day 100.

Also, you will be responsible for 20% for most covered services under Part B, 50% for outpatient mental health treatment, and a co-pay for outpatient hospital services.

> Tip: Medicare was never designed to pay for long-term care. In other words, if you will be living in a nursing home or if you will need around the clock care at home, Medicare does not pay for these services. Medicare is for acute, short term medical care and rehabilitative care only, otherwise called "skilled care".

Defining Skilled Care vs. Custodial Care

Skilled care is defined as care that is prescribed by a physician and performed by a licensed health care professional, like a nurse, physical therapist, or occupational therapist. Some examples of skilled care include: some wound care, IV antibiotics, or physical therapy immediately after a stroke.

Custodial care is another term for private pay care. This type of care can be performed by home health aids or other unlicensed caregivers, like family members. Some examples of custodial care include bathing, dressing, transferring from the bed to a chair, or toileting.

A Medicare Supplement policy will only cover some or all of the deductibles described above. This is a policy that you will have to purchase separately. Medicare supplements will not pay for (custodial) long-term care costs. They simply cover the deductibles under Medicare and sometimes pay for a few extras.

Long-Term Care Insurance will not cover Medicare deductibles like a Medicare Supplement policy will, but long-term care insurance will pay for all of the costs associated with long-term (custodial) nursing home care, in-home care, assisted living, and adult day care.

Medicare Supplements

Medicare Supplements, often referred to as Medigap plans, are purchased through private insurance companies to help fill the "gaps" that Medicare leaves behind. Medicare Supplements pick up the co-pays and deductibles associated with standard Medicare. There are ten standardized plans available labeled "A" through "J". Each plan has a different set of benefits. Medicare Supplements also do not cover the cost of long-term care; they simply pay deductibles and co-pays that Medicare does not.

Medicare HMOs
(a.k.a. Medicare Advantage or Medicare+Choice)

HMOs are Health Maintenance Organizations. An HMO will require that the participant use certain doctors and hospital systems in their area. HMOs are also for short acute care stays in hospitals, and for short rehabilitative stays in skilled nursing facilities. They do not pay for the cost of long-term care.

Private Insurance

Private health insurance through an employer or previous employer is essentially the same as HMOs, as far as coverage. Standard health insurance, no matter how great the benefit, *will ultimately not cover long-term care*.

Disability Insurance

Disability insurance covers household expenses, and is designed as income replacement. It will pay for things like groceries, rent and utilities. This insurance was not designed to cover the added expense of long-term care.

Veteran's Administration Benefits

Many Veterans mistakenly believe that when they need long-term care, their VA benefits will pay the expense. VA benefits for long-term care

are available, but the majority of those benefits are reserved for people with service connected disabilities. Check with your local VA office for more information.

VA Home Aid and Attendant Services Grant

There are financial benefits available for Veterans or their surviving spouses for non-service connected disabilities.

The Veterans Administration has established a pension program whereby your purchase of personal care and attendant home services may be paid for through your acquired pension. If you are a Veteran or the surviving spouse of a Veteran who has served at least 90 days or more on active duty with **one** day beginning or ending during a period of war, and you are in need of assistance at HOME due to your disabilities, you may be eligible for VA's non-service connected disability pension.

The following are the VA's defined "periods of war":

- WWI – 4/16/1917 to 11/11/1918
- WWII – 12/7/1941 to 12/31/1946
- Korea – 6/25/1950 to 1/31/1955
- Vietnam – 8/5/1964 to 5/7/1975
- Persian Gulf – 8/2/90 to present

Income and liquid assets are also a determination of eligibility. In 2006, if the veteran has assets in their own name below $80,000 (if married) or below $50,000 (if single) they may qualify. The car and house does not count as an asset. The Aid and Attendance income threshold for a veteran without dependents is now $18,234 annually. The threshold increases to $21,615 if a veteran has one dependent, and by $1,866 for each additional dependent. The annual Aid and Attendance threshold for a surviving spouse alone is $11,715. This threshold increases to $13,976 if there is one dependent child, and by $1,866 for each additional child.

As of 01/01/2007, a Veteran is eligible for up to $1,519 per month, while a surviving spouse is eligible for up to $976 per month. A couple is eligible for up to $1,801 per month.

In many cases if a person has a paid caregiver such as a nurse's aide, or they pay an Assisted Living Facility, those expenses impact so greatly on a person's net income, that they will meet the criteria for the income level.

If a Veteran or Veteran Widow has cash assets above the limit, they are allowed to place those assets into certain investments in order to have them "sheltered". This sheltering does not have a penalty or "look back period" associated with it. Proper asset sheltering for Aid and Attendance should be done under the supervision of an eldercare professional (Geriatric Care Managers can be found at *www.caremanager.org*), or Elder Law Attorney (*www.naela.org*) well versed in Medicaid planning because *one could easily ruin the chances of ever getting Medicaid if the VA pension planning was done incorrectly.*

With a little professional planning, many Veterans and Veteran Widows can receive pensions that make a significant difference in the amount of care they receive. After all, the reason for this particular pension is to assure that a Veteran or Veteran Widow does not live in a substandard environment in their old age. It takes a little work to apply for this pension, but anything worth having usually does.

Although you can apply on your own, it's best to seek the advice of a professional. Many in-home care agencies are familiar with this program and can assist with the completion of paperwork as well. *There is no fee to apply and find out if you or a loved one is entitled to these services.*

One of the best websites with comprehensive information can be found at www.veteranaid.org .

TIP: Additional information and assistance in applying for the Aid and Attendance benefit may be obtained by calling 1-800-827-1000. Applications may be submitted on-line at www.vabenefits.vba.va.gov/vonapp/main.asp. Information is also available on the Internet at www.va.gov or from any local veterans' service organization.

SENIOR SOLUTION #4

Understand What Applying for Medicaid Really Means —Before You Apply

Medicaid Defined

Medicaid was established by federal law (Title XIX of the Social Security Act), and is administered by each state individually. Medicaid is a program for poor or "impoverished" people, and people with high medical costs. Congress established Medicaid to provide a "safety net" for people who had no other way to pay for their health care or long-term care.

Medicaid is the long-term care payer of last resort for the frail elderly, persons with health problems, persons with mental retardation, mental illness, and those with physical or developmental disabilities.

Most long-term care and services such as prescription drugs, eyeglasses and dental care are provided at each state's discretion. When state money is scarce these services may be the most vulnerable, not because of ill will on the part of the state decision makers, but because there may be nowhere else to cut state budgets.

Medicaid is a highly flawed program, and is under-funded and over-burdened. States continue to make, and change, decisions about

Medicaid that among other things, will affect the amount of long-term care assistance available in each state, the eligibility criteria and number of persons eligible for that assistance, and the types of services that will be reimbursed.

The Deficit Reduction Act 2005

President George W. Bush signed The Deficit Reduction Omnibus Reconciliation Act of 2005 on February 8, 2006. The new law tightens Medicaid long term care eligibility rules and allows for the nationwide expansion of the Long Term Care (LTC) Partnership program.

This is great news for the long term care insurance industry as it will encourage proper planning for future long term care needs, and allow for the sale of Qualified State Long-Term Care Insurance policies (QSLTCI) under the new partnership program.

Changes to Medicaid Eligibility

The changes to Medicaid eligibility will make it harder for individuals to qualify for coverage. Such changes include:

Extension of look-back period for the transfer of assets from three years to five years prior to applying for Medicaid coverage. Note on grandfathering: The five-year look-back period will be phased in, as it will only affect transfers made after the law's effective date.

Applicants will need to meet the required spend-down limits prior to the start of their penalty period (if they have a penalty period).

Legislation will deny Medicaid coverage for nursing home care to any applicant with home equity valued above $500,000 (up to $750,000 in some states).

Expansion of Partnership Long-Term Care Insurance Policies

The new law also includes the expansion and availability of LTCI partnership plans nationally. Each individual state will have the opportunity to implement a Partnership program. Partnership policies help to protect state Medicaid budgets by requiring that the benefits of those qualifying insurance policies be paid before Medicaid benefits can be accessed. (The four existing partnership programs in CA, CT, IN, and NY will be grandfathered).

The new partnership policies allow consumers to protect a portion of their assets that they would typically need to spend down prior to qualifying for Medicaid coverage—ensuring that more of the funds accumulated for retirement will be protected.

Under the expansion of state partnerships, states must have the same requirements for partnership and non-partnership policies. The objective as states elect to participate is to have uniform requirements. Essentially, any tax-qualified LTCI policy approved by a state insurance department that meets the requirements of the federal partnership program would qualify for asset protection, on a dollar-for-dollar basis, up to the policy maximum.

Assets that must be spent down in order to qualify for Medicaid include:

- Cash
- Checking/ saving accounts
- CDs
- Savings bonds
- Investment accounts/mutual funds/ stocks
- IRA's and other retirement accounts
- Vacation homes and investment properties
- Second car
- Certain real estate or personal property not in use.

Assets that a person can keep or purposes of qualifying for Medicaid include:

- A home, (a principal residence with equity under $500,000)
- Household goods
- Personal effects
- Automobile—one per household
- Life insurance (no more than $1500 in cash surrender value)
- Prepaid burial plan and space or designated life insurance policy up to $1500.00
- Property essential to the individual's self support (perhaps a small business).
- Income producing property—other than cash, with some restrictions (like farmed land).

Reverse Mortgages and Medicaid

Reverse Mortgages do not affect Medicare (including Medicare Part D) or social security income. However, the proceeds from a reverse mortgage CAN affect local income based programs in your area, and the big one —Medicaid.

The first thing to remember is that aging adults should answer a lot of questions regarding their plans for the cash flow, or lump sum received from a reverse mortgage.

- Are they already in poor health?
- Do they intend to "gift" the money away to relatives?
- Are they using the money to pay for in-home care?
- Do they have long-term care insurance already?
- Are they planning on applying for Medicaid anytime soon?

If the answer to any of these questions is *yes*, they would be well advised to consult a local elder law attorney. (*www.naela.org*) Keep in mind, that *most elder law attorneys need education about reverse mortgages*. An aging adult may also be wise to consider having a son, daughter or other advocate accompany them when consulting an attorney.

The bottom line is that if someone needs to be on Medicaid soon, or are already there, then "gifting" and additional cash flow in their checking accounts or savings accounts can knock them out of eligibility quickly!

If your family member is thinking about taking the "lump sum" option available through a reverse mortgage, you might ask them to consider leaving the money in the *line of credit*. When they make a withdrawal from the line of credit (to pay bills, buy a new appliance, fix the air conditioner or heater) they must spend that money the same month that the withdrawal from the line of credit hits their checking account, and even then they need to keep receipts for service and goods purchased to prove that they didn't give the money away.

If that extra cash flow sits in their checking or savings account for more than 30 days, it could knock them out of eligibility.

If a senior decides that they want to receive the monthly check to increase their cash flow, they should make sure that they need the money every month to pay bills. If that checking account starts adding up, or if they are above the allowed amount of income because of the additional cash flow, they may be getting into trouble.

Don't assume that your family member knows the rules, because the rules are complicated and change regularly. Talk to someone who knows and studies these laws all the time.

Prenuptial Agreements

For second marriages this information is particularly important.

"What's mine is mine, what's his is his. They won't touch MY money for HIS long-term care, right?"

Yes, they will. Prenuptial agreements hold no weight when it comes to Medicaid. When two people are married, their assets become marital property. So even if Nancy has $1 million dollars, and Robert has

$5,000 dollars, is doesn't really matter. If one of them needs care, and they have no long-term care insurance, they will have to go through the spend-down process considering both of their combined assets.

Mandatory Estate Recovery

With the changes in federal law enacted in August 1993, the state must seek recovery of Medicaid expenditures from the estate of a *deceased individual* who was 55 or older when he or she received assistance.

This means that when the person on Medicaid dies, the state will collect the amount they spent on that person's care from the remaining estate. The state must include all real estate and personal property and other assets included within an estate under the state's probate law. The state may include other property in which the individual had an interest at the time of death. If the deceased Medicaid recipient has a spouse still living in the home (community spouse), that spouse can usually continue living in the home until his or her death, before the state will seek recovery. Usually a Medicaid lien is placed on the property of the Medicaid recipient.

Transferring Assets

"I'll just give it all away!"

When a person applies for Medicaid to pay for medical care, federal law requires the state to consider recent transfers of assets and monetary gifts. If a person or his or her spouse has transferred assets for less than fair market value in the 60 months (5 years) prior to applying for Medicaid, or at any time after applying, the applicant will be considered "ineligible" for a period of time based on the amount transferred. In the case of assets transferred to a "trust" the look back period is the same, 60 months. The look back period means that the state can go back 5 years and see if any transfers have been made and add them (based on a specific calculation) to the ineligibility period.

SENIOR SOLUTION #4

Divorce

If Robert and Nancy had given $120,000 to their wonderful daughter Susan, for safe keeping 6 years prior to Robert's stroke, Robert would almost immediately be eligible for Medicaid.

But what if Susan's husband Scott decided that he wanted a divorce? Technically, in most states that money would be considered marital property and would be divided in half, leaving Susan with only $60,000 of her parent's money.

Lawsuits

Susan has her parent's $120,000 in a bank account in her and her husband's names. Husband Scott is in a car accident, and the other party sues Scott for damages beyond what his insurance company will pay. The plaintiff's lawyer sees $120,000 sitting in their account. If he wins the case, they may lose it all.

Financial Aid

Susan and Scott have a daughter who will be 18 in a few months. She is looking forward to going away to college. The family applies for financial aid, but because they have Susan's parent's $120,000 in their account, their daughter does not qualify for financial aid.

Buying Toys

Susan and Scott have always been fairly responsible, but have decided that they need that new boat. Susan's parents, Robert and Nancy won't know if they borrow just $20,000. The kids will be sure to pay it back…eventually.

SENIOR SOLUTION #5

Using a Reverse Mortgage to Keep Mom and Dad at Home Longer Might Be the Best Option

Reverse Mortgages (Home Equity Conversion Mortgages) have become a popular and well respected way for seniors to access the equity in their homes for many reasons. Some use the equity for long-term care needs, to pay bills, pay off existing mortgages or debt, pay for prescription drug costs, home improvements, home modifications, or to simply be able to enjoy life a little more by traveling and enhancing their retirement cash flow. Many seniors use reverse mortgages to pay high property tax bills, and have even been saved from foreclosure and bankruptcy because they applied for a reverse mortgage.

Other seniors use reverse mortgage proceeds to fund advanced estate planning techniques. This includes increasing the value of their estate through life insurance purchases, planning ahead for future long-term care needs, assisting grandchildren with college funding, making charitable donations, and to convert IRA funds to Roth IRA funds, just to name a few.

Many newspaper, TV, radio and internet articles circulating in the media give inaccurate and misleading information about reverse mortgages. So called "experts" who are interviewed for quotes often have no involvement in the mortgage industry and do not understand the federal law that regulates these loans.

Each consumer should make it his or her own responsibility to talk with an expert, and educate themselves on the facts.

> TIP: As you know, the media attract more viewers, readers and listeners when they make a story exciting, scary or dramatic. Because reverse mortgages are federally regulated loans, there really isn't anything scary or dramatic about them when you know the facts. Be wary of interviews and articles that make reverse mortgages seem like a scam. The Department of Housing and Urban Development has done an excellent job of regulating reverse mortgages, and they are designed to help seniors not hurt them.

Some good websites for more information are www.fanniemae.com—be sure to download "Money from Home" for free. The National Reverse Mortgage Lenders Association has great consumer booklets—www.reversemortgage.org.

The National Council on Aging recently did a study that concluded that reverse mortgages are good sources of funds for long-term care planning and long-term care needs. You can download the entire study by visiting www.ncoa.org.

Although there are closing costs associated with these loans, most, if not all of them are factored in to the loan, and are not out-of-pocket expenses for the senior. Whether or not a reverse mortgage is right for a senior depends on their specific situation, and cash flow or estate planning needs.

What is a (HECM) Reverse Mortgage?

A reverse mortgage enables older homeowners (62+) to convert part of the equity in their homes into tax-free income without having to sell the home, give up title, or take on a new monthly mortgage payment. The reverse mortgage is aptly named because the payment stream is "reversed." Instead of making monthly payments to a lender, as with a regular mortgage, a lender makes payments to you.

Who Qualifies for a Reverse Mortgage?

Eligible property types include single-family homes, 2-4 unit properties, manufactured homes (built after June 1976), condominiums, and townhouses. As long as you own a home, are at least 62, and have enough equity in your home, you can get a reverse mortgage. There are no special income, credit or medical requirements.

How Are Seniors Protected?

Counseling is one of the most important consumer protections built into the program. It requires an independent third-party to make sure the senior understands the program, and review alternative options, before they apply for a reverse mortgage.

You can seek counseling from a local HUD-approved counseling agency, or a national counseling agency such as AARP (800-209-8085), National Foundation for Credit Counseling (866-698-6322), and Money Management International (877-908-2227). Counseling is required for all reverse mortgages and may be conducted face-to-face or by telephone.

By law, a counselor must review: (i) options, other than a reverse mortgage, that are available to the prospective borrower, including housing, social services, health and financial alternatives; (ii) other home equity conversion options that are or may become available to the prospective borrower, such as property tax deferral programs; (iii) the financial implications of entering into a reverse mortgage; and, (iv) the tax consequences affecting the prospective borrower's eligibility under state or federal programs and the impact on the estate and his or her heirs.

> TIP: HUD Counselors are not financial planners, and should not be giving advice on financial product purchases. Talk to a trusted advisor about a plan for the reverse mortgage proceeds.

How Can the Cash Flow From a Reverse Mortgage Keep Mom and Dad at Home Longer?

The cash flow from a reverse mortgage can be used for any purpose. In order to keep seniors safe and at home for longer periods of time, it is recommended that the cash flow be used for home modifications, repairs, personal emergency response systems, and in-home care services.

Does the Senior's Name Remain on the Title to the Home?

The seniors' names remain on the title to the home. The bank is not in the business of taking over title, and certainly not in the business of owning homes. Therefore, just as with a traditional mortgage, the senior's name is on the title to the house.

Can Their Home Be Taken Away from Them?

When a senior implements a reverse mortgage, it is important to remember that they are responsible for keeping the home owner's insurance in force, paying annual property taxes, and for general upkeep of the home. Unless one of these criteria is not met, their home can never be taken away from them.

Will Heirs Be Responsible for Repaying This Loan?

No, a reverse mortgage is a "non-recourse" loan. This means that the lender is only entitled to loan repayment via the sale of the home for fair market value. If there is any remaining equity over and above the final loan amount, the heirs receive that remaining equity. If the home sells for LESS than the final loan amount, the federal government steps in and pays the lender the difference. Heirs' assets are never at risk.

When Does the Loan Come Due?

The loan comes due when the last remaining homeowner leaves the home permanently. This means that the loan will come due when the last homeowner passes away, sells the home, or leaves permanently (12 months or more).

Can Mom and Dad Still Leave Their Home to Their Children?

Yes, with proper planning they certainly can. One way to make sure that heirs receive the value of the home is for the seniors to purchase life insurance using the proceeds from the reverse mortgage. Some seniors end up doubling or tripling the value of their estate for their heirs because they use the reverse mortgage proceeds to pay the life insurance premiums. This way they never have to touch a penny of their savings, investments, or current income to increase the value of their own estate. This also helps the heirs, because inheritance passed on through life insurance (beneficiary designation) bypasses probate and taxes!

How Does the Deficit Reduction Act of 2005 Affect Home Equity?

The Deficit Reduction Act of 2005 requires that individuals with home equity over $500,000 ($750,000 in some states) use some of that equity to pay for their own care prior to qualifying for Medicaid services. Reverse mortgages have become a very popular and appropriate option for decreasing the equity in the home and using that equity to pay for care.

True Stories of Seniors Whose Lives and Homes Were Saved

Thousands of Seniors Face Losing Their Homes Without Assistance!

(Florida, 2006): Freddie is a 78-year-old mother of six, who has lived in her home for over 40 years. She is challenged with reading and writing. She received a "foreclosure notice" from her current mortgage holder because of late payments. Her son contacted Roy Shellhammer, with Next Generation Financial Services www.ngfs.net, in February of 2006 to discuss a Reverse Mortgage.

The current mortgage holder was uncommunicative and very difficult to work with, continuing to add on additional charges and fees to her current loan. When NGFS finally had a closing date set with an appropriate closing amount, and closing documents, the mortgage holder suggested to Freddie and her family that they should apply for a hardship reduction in fees.

She started this process with NGFS support. The mortgage holder would not respond to requests for a new payoff figure. The interest rate lock was lost (interest rates on reverse mortgages change weekly per HUD) and now the fees were greater than the amount of outside funds available. It appeared as if Freddie would lose her home.

Freddie's family contacted a local "legal aid" group, and they put in a tremendous amount of effort to get the mortgage holder to provide a payoff figure. The mortgage holder denied the hardship reduction. The legal aid had to petition a judge to require the mortgage holder to provide the necessary information. The lawyers finally were able to talk the day before closing.

1st Mariner Bank, along with the assistance of Financial Freedom Inc. honored the original interest rate on the reverse mortgage (they certainly didn't have to!); Resource Services (title company) supported multiple changes to closing documents and dates; and Kelly Polizotto and the NGFS staff pro-

SENIOR SOLUTION #5

vided professional service and extreme patience beyond the processing of a Reverse Mortgage transaction.

Freddie closed her Reverse Mortgage on 07/21/2006 and may live in her home the rest of her life, PAYMENT FREE.

With the help of the Reverse Mortgage, and with some assistance from family and friends, her church, legal aid, and loan consultants Roy Shellhammer, Troy Shellhammer, and Grant Shellhammer, Freddie's home was saved, but not without a lot of hard work from everyone involved!

Next Generation Financial Services is a division of 1st Mariner Bank, offering reverse mortgages nationwide. Roy, Troy, and Grant Shellhammer are loan consultants located in Longwood, Florida. They can be reached for comment at 888.9REVERSE, or at their website www.rtgconsultants.com or www.reversemortgagenation.com .

SENIOR SOLUTION #6

Surrounding Yourself/ Your Family With a Team of Experts is the Best Medicine

Financial Advisors Helping Seniors with Cash Flow Planning

Most financial advisors can help with products like life insurance, long-term care insurance, annuities, and IRAs or 401Ks. Not all financial advisors are able to incorporate reverse mortgages and cash flow planning techniques into seniors' estate planning strategies. When it comes to estate planning and long-term care planning, or crisis management it is important to seek the advice of an individual who is well versed and trained in not only senior issues, but also reverse mortgages and cash flow planning techniques.

Finding a Trusted Advisor Who Can Help

One way to find a trusted advisor who possesses all of these skills is to visit *www.reversemortgagenation.com* and search for a financial advisor in your state.

Elder Law Attorneys

Aging adults and their family members face certain challenging legal issues. Issues such as legal matters, financial matters, and care planning can be complicated for seniors, as well as for their family. Once again, expert legal help is often the key to solving many problems and avoiding future complexities. It is important to be able to identify a competent Elder Law Attorney who can assist the family in a timely and professional manner. Consumers should be cautious and check credentials thoroughly.

The leading national organization of Elder Law Attorneys is the National Academy of Elder Law Attorneys (NAELA), on the web at: *www.naela.org*. Membership is open to any lawyer, but the membership does show that at least the attorney has some interest in the field. Other sources to consider are referrals from family and friends, and referrals from other professionals such as social workers and medical professionals who work in long-term care. Ask the attorney how many nursing home cases they handle each month. It is likely that the attorney who does four Medicaid cases per month is more up to date than the attorney who does four per year.

> TIP: Many elder law attorneys are not well versed in reverse mortgages. Speak with a financial professional who has been trained in this area of planning. www.reversemortgagenation.com

Geriatric Care Management as a Resource

When faced with decisions regarding long-term care for an aging loved one, a geriatric care manager may be one of the best private resources in your area. A geriatric care manager has extensive knowledge of all local resources related to aging and caregiving, as well as family and personal issues and concerns.

Geriatric care managers can be located nationwide. They assist with coordination of care for aging and disabled adults. This service is provided in a series of steps including initial assessment, care plan development, implementation of services, and quality of care monitoring. Geriatric care managers are typically nurses, social workers, gerontologists, physical therapists, occupational therapists, or other social service professionals.

The "care management" process can improve the quality of life not only for the aging adult, but also for the caregivers and family members involved. The service is very personalized and utilizes the same principals of "case management."

Most geriatric care managers are available to the family and client 24 hours per day, 7 days per week. The ultimate goal is to keep the aging adult in the home for as long as **safely** possible. In-home care can be arranged at any level of need to accommodate the client and the family. Geriatric care managers often will be asked to arrange other services for the client such as bill paying, housekeeping, lawn care, transportation to appointments, grocery shopping, meal delivery, and personal care issues.

When the client is in need of transition to alternative living arrangements like nursing home, assisted living, or even independent retirement communities, the care manager often can recommend the best facilities that meet the clients financial needs.

Geriatric Care Management is truly a holistic approach to caring for the aging adult. All resources available are utilized to assist families when long-term care is needed.

Care managers are also often asked to troubleshoot quality concerns with nursing homes and home care agencies. Their level of professionalism and knowledge of the local regulations and laws are of great value to the family. They are considered "advocates" for the elderly.

Geriatric care management is paid for privately by client and family members. Medicare and Medicaid do not cover these services. However, Long-Term Care Insurance does cover some or all of the care management fee.

Most geriatric care managers belong to the National Association of Professional Geriatric Care Managers. In order to find a care manager in your area, you can search for one through their website at *www.caremanager.org*

In the Midwest, you can search for a local care manager at *www.midwestgcm.org*, or for an example of a specific care management website, try *www.theltcexpert.com*.

Geriatric care management services save the family both time and money, and ultimately decrease the stress and frustration of the caregiver. The process gives the family and the aging adult the opportunity to make informed and appropriate decisions regarding any long-term care needs.

Recommendations for Choosing a Geriatric Care Manager

Choosing a geriatric care manager is much like choosing any other professional that you and your family would be working with closely.

- Look for a member of the National Association of Professional Geriatric Care Managers. These members have met certain criteria regarding education and experience in health sciences and social service.
- Ask for References.
- Ask for literature about their company, years of practice, websites, and biography.
- Check with the Better Business Bureau.
- Ask about fees, contracts, and extra charges like mileage or phone calls.
- Be sure you understand what services they provide and their on-call schedule. Will they be available 24 hours a day?
- Remember that a geriatric care manager becomes your "eyes and ears," especially when you live some distance from your parents.

SENIOR SOLUTION #6

Ask them about their process, their communication schedule (Will they report daily, weekly, or monthly?). Is the primary communication via telephone or email?

- Communicate any concerns immediately, and work together as a team to accomplish the ultimate goal, which is keeping your loved one safe and well cared for.

My Parent Doesn't Want Any Help, What Should I Do?

Perhaps you have noticed that Mom or Dad isn't bathing regularly, or the bills aren't being paid, or the house is uncharacteristically messy. Maybe they seem to forget directions from one location to anther, or even worse, they have had a car accident, or report falling in the home when no one was around to help them. Often adult children of aging parents notice changes in their loved ones, and when the aging adult is confronted with the facts, they say, "Oh everything is fine, I don't need any help, don't worry about me!"

The loss of independence and choice is something no one wants to face. Having one's own children tell their parents what do to or how to live their lives is uncomfortable at best. Many aging adults are also very private about their financial matters, and will not discuss income, expenses, or assets with adult children.

How does an adult child start that conversation with their parents? There is not a one-size-fits-all answer. Below are some tips that might help the process along.

- Choose an appropriate time and place. Avoid large family gatherings, holidays, birthdays, and other celebrations. A quiet location, in their home or yours, might be more comfortable.

- Avoid blaming or accusing. Instead, redirect the conversation by telling your parent how YOU feel. For example, "Mom, I find myself worrying about you a lot these days, and I would like to tell you why I am feeling this way."

- Talk to a geriatric care manager in your area for some good advice on how to approach your parent's specific needs. That care manager has helped family members have this kind of conversation hundreds of times throughout their career. They are full of helpful hints and tips.

- If you decide to seek the services of a geriatric care manager, ask them about their approach when it comes to dealing with difficult clients or clients who may not perceive a need for services.

- Advice for adult children when approaching their parents about setting up an evaluation, might include telling their parents, "I know you don't want me to worry about you, and I only want the best for you. Having this professional come over and talk to us would really make me feel better. If you would agree to talk with her, we can look at her recommendations together and see if any of them make sense. Is that fair?"

- Remember that having a third party, who is not a family member and is completely objective, can help the senior see things from a different point of view. They feel like they are getting some professional advice as opposed to opinions from their children.

- Finally, if the senior is truly not living safely, a geriatric care manager can let the senior know that they need to make some choices about their care or living arrangements NOW, before someone else has to make that decision for them later. Of course this is done with professionalism, courtesy, compassion and caring.

SENIOR SOLUTION #7

Attention Adult Children and Family Members Caring for an Aging Adult— Give Yourself a Break

When the Caregiver Needs a Break... Where Can They Turn?

One out of four families in the U.S. today are caring for an aging adult in some way. For some families that means 24-hour live-in care. For other families that means that Mom needs a ride to the doctor or to the grocery.

In the next 10-20 years it is projected that elder care will replace childcare as the number one issue for working adults. Employers will likewise be affected.

Caring for an aging parent can be rewarding and overwhelming at the same time. After all, these are ones parents who raised us and cared for us. It's very difficult when the roles reverse.

Respite (*res*-pit) care is often the answer. Respite care is *time off* for the caregiver. Respite gives the caregiver time away to rest and do necessary activities so that they can continue to provide good care for their loved one. Often being a caregiver is a job that can be physically and emotionally draining. Without relief a person's physical and emotional health can be affected, reducing the quality of care for their family member. There are several options when it comes to respite care.

In-home care can be arranged for as little as a few hours, up to several days with the proper planning and financial resources. Be sure to pick an agency with a great reputation and proven reliability. Make sure that background checks are done on all employees and Elder/Child Abuse checks are also completed. In-home care for long periods of time can be costly, so be sure to budget for the expense. Also many home health agencies require several days or weeks of advance notice for long assignments. Plan ahead

Nursing Home/ Assisted Living facilities often will offer respite care for a weekend or a full week or more. Many facilities have a minimum number of days required. The cost includes room and board. Many other services will be extra. Some facilities will only require a few days notice, and others will require several weeks notice. Check with the facilities in your area for costs and bed availability. Again, as always it is important to plan ahead.

Local Area Agencies on Aging or Social Service Agencies will sometimes sponsor programs that allow for volunteers to come to the home and provide respite care for short periods of time. These visits are usually just for a few hours. The volunteers are not medical professionals and therefore are not able to care for seriously ill family members, but they are able to provide some relief! These programs are usually free or at a very low cost to local residents. Contact your local Area Agency on Aging for more information.

The Alzheimer's Association is a great source of information. It is not necessary to be taking care of an Alzheimer's diagnosed family member to take advantage of their referral database. Your local agency can usually provide you with a wealth of information, resources and contacts.

Family and friends are a great resource for the caregiver. Don't be afraid to ask for help. Many people are happy to assist with errand running and caregiving. Have a family meeting and ask each family member for 1-2 hours of his or her time per week. This will allow the caregiver to take a hot bath, read a book, go for a much-needed walk, or just go shopping. Make a schedule and give each family member a copy.

Local Churches and Other Organizations are generally willing to send volunteers out to the home for a few hours. Again, most of these volunteers are non-medical personnel and will only be able to stay for a couple of hours at a time.

Taking care of yourself is just as important as caring for your disabled/aging family member. If you become ill, what will happen to your loved one? Don't hesitate to ask for help. If you look in the right places you might find more help than you need.

So take a much-needed break. You deserve it!

Hospice Care—At The End of Life

Hospice care is end of life care. Usually it is estimated by a physician that a patient has 6 months or less to live. Hospice focuses on caring for the individual, keeping them comfortable, and providing support for the family. Hospice care can be provided in the home, in a designated hospice facility, or in a long-term care facility. These services are available to patients of all ages. It is covered under Medicare, Medicaid, and most private insurance plans. Long-Term Care Insurance also covers hospice care.

The primary caregiver for a hospice patient is usually a family member. There is a team of healthcare professionals available to help the primary caregiver. This team often includes a physician, a registered nurse, home health aids, clergy or social services, trained volunteers, and physical or occupational therapists. Traditional insurance plans like Medicare and private health insurance will cover needed supplies, equipment, and licensed healthcare practitioners like nurses and physical therapists. However when a family needs 24 hour care provided by a home health aid, or other unlicensed personnel, they end up paying privately for this service or utilize their long-term care insurance benefits. Most long-term care insurers provide hospice care as a standard benefit in their plan and there is no need to meet the waiting period (elimination period).

Pay Yourself or a Loved One for Providing Care— The Options and Tax Benefits

Many adult children find it financially impossible to leave their current employer and give up a much needed salary to take care of an aging adult. There are some ways to offset that financial responsibility, but it does take diligence and investigation the part of the adult child.

Seniors can pay adult children or other care providers just like they would a home health agency for services. *Increasing cash flow for the senior to afford to pay privately for care can be done through a reverse mortgage.*

Some seniors have *long-term care insurance* that allows a family member to be the primary caregiver, and get reimbursed for providing the care.

If neither of those options apply, here are some other options:

- If employed, check with you company's human resource department or seek the counsel of your employee assistance program to find out about family leave options or local programs that assist with caregiving expenses and options.
- Contact Eldercare Locator, as service of the National Association of Area Agencies on Aging at *www.n4a.org/locator* or phone 800-677-1116.
- A state by state listing of paid leave programs for caregivers can be found at *www.paidfamilyleave.org*

Some other examples that offer at least some level of compensation for caregiving family members include:

- *Colorado:* In rural areas, family members providing assistance to loved ones may be eligible to receive up to $400 per month as compensation to provide personal care services.
- *North Dakota:* pays up to $700 per month to spouses and other family members who care for Medicaid beneficiaries living in rural areas who would otherwise require admission to a nursing home.
- *Wisconsin:* a family member may be eligible for compensation either for caregiving or, in some situations, for performing services normally provided by a social worker.
- *North Carolina:* family caregivers supporting loved ones may be able to reduce out of pocket expenses through the use of state-funded vouchers that can be used to buy nutritional supplements, incontinence supplies, and personal emergency response systems, among other items. In some circumstances caregivers may be eligible for direct cash compensation. While in most cases compensation is provided to family members who are not immediate family, there are times when immediate family is eligible for pay, such as when they are caring for a loved one with dementia who lives in a rural area.
- *Massachusetts:* Elders who meet Medicaid criteria and who qualify for nursing home care now have the option of receiving compensated home-based care from family members or friends. The Enhanced Adult Foster Program covers up to $18,000 annually for family members who provide 24-hour care in the home. These caregivers receive specialized training, support of both a registered nurse and a care manager, and help in locating respite services.

Tax Deductions and Benefits for Caregivers

There are certain criteria that must be met if a family caregiver is planning to claim an aging parent as a dependent.

- You must provide more than half of a person's financial support.

- The dependent may be a relative or non-relative living with you for the entire year or residing in a nursing home or assisted living home.
- They (the dependent) must be a citizen of the U.S., Canada, or Mexico.
- The dependent must not file a joint tax return for the same year.
- The dependent must have less than $3,200 of gross annual income. Social Security benefits and tax exempt interest income are not included in this equation (neither would reverse mortgage proceeds, as they are not taxable).

Qualifying expenses include:

- medications
- long-term care insurance premiums
- home modifications
- transportation for medical appointments
- services of privately hired in-home care workers
- spending for wheelchairs, eye glasses, and dentures
- Look for anything related to meeting the long-term care needs of the individual! Any expense not covered by insurance may be eligible for deductions.
- For those residing in an assisted living facility, there may be a certain percentage allowed as deductible.
- For those residing in a nursing home—and *paying privately* for their care, the cost is fully deductible.

It's important to consult the advice of a tax advisor or elder law attorney, especially if the support gets complicated—for instance:

- When multiple siblings contribute to the support of a parent.
- When taxable income could be moved into tax-free investments.
- When there is the possibility that the dependent may need to apply for Medicaid.

- When a caregiver contract is desired to provide family members with compensation for services, housing, etc.
- If you hired someone to care for your loved one while you either sought or maintained employment, you may qualify for the Child and Dependent Care Credit. Depending on your income, this credit may equal up to 35% of your qualifying expenses. To claim the credit, the following conditions must be met:
- You must have earned income wages, salaries, tips, employee compensation or net earnings from self-employment.
- Payments for care cannot be made to any person you claim as a dependent or to your child under age 19.
- You must file as single, head of household, qualified widow(er) with a dependent child, or married filing jointly.
- The care must have been provided by a qualifying individual.
- The dependent must have lived with you for more than half of the year.

Remember to consult a local tax consultant for more help, information, and possible state level deductions in your area.

Talk to Employers About Dependent Care FSAs

Consider utilizing a Dependent Care FSA (Flexible Spending Accounts) to help pay for medical/elder care expenses. These plans allow employees to contribute a portion of salary, before taxes, to accounts designated for health care expenses, including premiums and child/elder care expenses. Then employees are reimbursed from their accounts with tax free dollars for unreimbursed medical expenses and child/elder care expenses. The funds must be used before the end of the plan year, or grace period, or else unused dollars are forfeited. If a caregiver has access to these plans, they should use them, but plan carefully so that contributions are not more than can be used in a year.

If an elderly parent lives with a participant and relies on that person for at least 50% of their support, then the Dependent Care FSA may be used for day care expenses. However, the care must be necessary to allow the participant to work, and cannot be custodial nursing care. Also, if the participant is married, the care must be necessary because the spouse also works, is looking for work or is a full-time student.

SENIOR SOLUTION #8

Living at Home is Possible, and A Lot Easier When You Know What Questions to Ask

Tips and Hints for Choosing In-Home Care Services

> TIP: For home care agencies that do care for Medicare patients, you can see their last state survey results by visiting www.medicare.gov. Remember, not all home care agencies take Medicare. Some are private pay only.

- Be organized.
- Ask the Home Care Agency if they have a back-up person on-call in case of caregivers becoming ill or not showing up.
- Provide the aide with a checklist of duties for EACH DAY.
- The aide should not sleep or smoke in your home.

- If there is a problem, immediately contact the agency that sent the aide.
- The aides should provide their own lunch/dinner unless you offer.
- Do not tip.
- Do not send your loved one out in a car with the aide unless this situation is prearranged with the agency.
- Aides should only *minimally* use the phone for personal calls.
- Make sure you know in advance how payment is expected.
- Some aides are Certified Nurse's Aides (CNAs) and others are not. Some will take a blood pressure and a pulse, while others will not. Ask the agency.
- There should be some consistency after about 1 to 2 weeks regarding the person who is sent to the home. Sometimes it takes a week or so to get the same person on the schedule for your home. Be patient!
- What is the hiring practice of the agency? Have background checks been performed on every caregiver? What about Elder Abuse or Child Abuse database checks? Are they bonded and insured?
- If there are too many late shows/no shows or inconsistencies, CHANGE AGENCIES (speak to them about the problem first, perhaps they can correct the situation).

Medical vs. Non-Medical Home Care Services

There are two different types of home care providers, *medical* and *non-medical*. A non-medical home care agency supplies caregivers who will do household chores such as light cleaning, laundry, errand running, grocery shopping, picking up prescriptions, light meal preparation, and getting the mail. They will also provide services that help with socialization and transportation like accompanying the aging adult to a doctor's appointment, sitting and watching TV together, playing card games or board games, taking the senior to special events or senior centers, going to the library, and other social activities. Again, transporting the senior in the caregiver's vehicle should be pre-approved.

Medical home care providers can assist with many of these things, but also provide bathing and dressing assistance, medication reminders, and assistance with transferring from the bed to a chair.

No one can take care of your parent or spouse exactly the way you would, but a good agency will provide caring and compassionate staff who do the best job they possibly can. The squeaky wheel always gets the grease when it comes to service providers. Do your homework prior to hiring an agency, and be sure to check on your aging loved one regularly. Visit unexpectedly and monitor what's happening in the home. Speak up and communicate with the agency!

Adult Day Care

Adult Day Care Centers are becoming a popular alternative to nursing home placement. They offer the ability for the elderly to spend the day in an enriching environment, full of social activities and learning opportunities, while interacting with others. Many Adult Day Centers will provide transportation to and from the center for an extra charge. Meals are provided, as well as medication administration. Day trips, crafts, computer stations, libraries, and music are often part of the overall experience. Some Adult Day Centers will take Medicaid, but most prefer private pay or long-term care insurance. This allows the senior to live at home with another member of the family, but have supervision and social interaction during the day while family members are at work.

Tips for Choosing an Adult Day Care Center

Identify services in your area. For names and phone numbers of the Adult Day Centers, try:

- Yellow Pages ("Adult Day Care;" "Aging Services;" Senior Citizens' Services," etc.).

- Area Agency on Aging (AAA). Call 1-800-677-1116 for the AAA in your area, or search for them online.
  - A local senior center.
  - Your family doctor.
  - A Geriatric Care Manager.
- Call first! Call Adult Day Centers and ask for a flier or brochure, eligibility criteria, a monthly activity calendar, a monthly menu and application procedures.
- Know what to ask. Look for the following information:
  - Owner or sponsoring agency.
  - Years of operation.
  - Openings and availability. Are they accepting new clients?
  - License or certification (if required in your state).
  - Hours of operation.
  - Days open.
  - Transportation.
  - Cost—Hourly or daily charge, other charges, financial assistance.
  - Medical conditions accepted— such as memory loss, limited mobility, and incontinence.
  - Staff credentials.
  - Number of staff per participant.
  - Activities provided—Is there variety and choice of individual and group activities?
  - Menu—appeal, balance.
- Tour. After reviewing materials, make an appointment to visit two or more centers that might meet your needs.
- Check references. Talk to two or three people who have used the center you are considering. Ask for their opinion.

- Try it out. Select a day center. Try it for three to five days. It sometimes takes several visits for new participants to feel comfortable in a new setting and with a new routine. If you have questions or are experiencing any problems, ask for a conference. The staff may have suggestions to make the transition easier both at home and at the day center.

Transportation Resources for Seniors

Americans are in love with their cars because having a driver's license is tied to one of America's core values—independence. We feel entitled to get in our vehicle and travel wherever we want whenever we choose, and we rely on our automobiles to access the outside world. But when individuals are told by their doctor that it's not safe to drive anymore or they lose their financial ability to maintain a car, one can experience a drastic decline in independence.

Older adults are especially vulnerable to losing their independence because of driving issues. When an individual (or a family member) determines that safety is an issue because of physical limitations or cognitive impairment, the transition from independence to inter-dependence is not always easy. The lack of independent transportation has been tied to self-care problems, isolation and loneliness. It is logical to assume that reduced mobility leads to a higher risk of poor health (less access to goods and services necessary for health and welfare) and depression. Those who stop driving usually rely on friends and family members for transportation but take fewer trips per week, and those trips revolve around the schedule and convenience of others.

In suburban or rural areas it is difficult to access grocery stores, restaurants, shopping malls, or entertainment centers because most destinations are often too far to walk, public transportation is poor or unavailable, taxis are too expensive, and special services are limited. Even if public transportation is available, often it is nearly impossible for an older adult to walk to the bus stop or train station, wait for the next arrival (without a resting place), hear the destination announcements, arrive safely, and then do everything successfully in reverse.

As the number of older adults continues to grow, we must assume the number of unsafe drivers on the roads will also increase. Just the other day, I had a conversation with an 83-year old woman who confided that her doctor had told her it is time to stop driving because of her macular degeneration. Instead of taking the doctor's advice, she said she was going to find another doctor!

Many times the safety of our older loved ones (and the safety of others) depends on family members addressing the issue. There are driver safety assessments available to measure driving skills and to identify the warning signs when someone should begin to limit driving or stop altogether. Go to *www.aarp.org/families/driver_safety* to test your driving IQ or the driving safety of your loved one.

If and when the time comes to give up driving altogether, one would hope there are alternatives provided by local communities. There are many resources posted on the internet (see attached) but finding services in your local area might be a challenge. In researching the information for this chapter, it is evident my suburban community has options for medical transportation, but very little service other than taxis for those who need to run errands, visit friends, or attend the theater. Because our county is spread over a wide area, taxis are sometimes too expensive for older adults on a fixed income. After some online research and a check of the yellow pages, I concluded that if there are transportation resources in my area, they have decided to keep their services a secret.

A new and creative model for "dignified transportation" is the Independent Transportation Network (*www.itnamerica.org*). The non-profit organization provides a way for local communities to establish a collaborative effort between individuals, family members, businesses, health care providers, and donors to provide independent, dignified transportation 24 hours a day, 7 days a week for those who cannot or should not drive anymore. It requires a membership fee and a pay as you go system, but volunteer drivers can earn transportation credits toward their future transportation needs. One volunteer described it as "transportation social security." After participating as a volunteer, he felt entitled to use the services for himself when he encountered a vision problem.

Planning for longevity is similar to making a career change—you must consider all facets of quality living; and having easy, accessible transportation is one of the most important factors to consider. As more attention is paid to "aging in place," more creative options for transportation are bound to be available as the demand grows.

The above information on transportation was contributed by Althea West, LTCP, Gerontologist, Senior Planning Consultant, 1-800-984-8407, *amw@arn-us.com*.

SENIOR SOLUTION #9

Alternative Living Arrangements Can Be a Positive Experience

Using a Reverse Mortgage to Pay for Home Improvements

Mom and Dad often want to stay in their own home, the home in which they have lived, raised their children in, and feel most comfortable. Often in order to safely stay in their current home, a senior's home will need modification and repair. These repairs and modifications can be expensive. Reverse mortgages can be used to pay for home improvements. These improvements in combination with a personal emergency response system and some in-home assistance can keep seniors in their own homes much longer. In older homes, doorways may need to be widened for wheelchair and walker accessibility, sinks and countertops can be lowered to a more manageable height, wheelchair ramps can be installed, along with safety bars in bathrooms and down long hallways. Many seniors need new heating and updated cooling systems in their homes as well. With increased demand for these senior-friendly features, more home builders and home improvement businesses are specializing in this area.

Continuum Of Care Retirement Communities (CCRC)

A CCRC is a community for seniors that encompasses all levels of care, from independent living, to assisted living, to nursing home care, all on one campus. Some couples and single seniors will move to a CCRC for various reasons including simplifying their lifestyle, no longer having to worry about lawn and house maintenance, and increased social activity with people of their own generation. Independent living offers an apartment or town-home with access to 1-2 meals per day in a restaurant style setting, recreational activities, group tours and day outings, and transportation to doctor appointments and grocery stores. They often include walking trails, workout rooms, arts and crafts areas, computer labs, libraries, chapels, and small convenience stores. The independent portion of a CCRC is not considered long-term care; it is simply a lifestyle choice. Independent senior living has a cost range of $1100-$5000 per month. Most cities do have Section 8 or HUD housing specifically for seniors. Sometimes there is a waiting list for subsidized housing.

Assisted Living Facilities

Sometimes, on the same campus there are assisted living facilities that offer most of the same accommodations, but with a little more assistance and structure. In an assisted living facility each resident typically has their own apartment, but without a kitchenette. They are served 3 meals per day in a family style or restaurant style setting. Medication delivery is available, as well as linen service, laundry service, housekeeping, and assistance with bathing and dressing if needed. Again, recreational and social activities, and transportation are also provided.

There are stand-alone assisted living facilities that are not associated with CCRCs. Assisted living is becoming the most popular form of long-term care, and is seen as a transition between independent living and nursing home care. This is a nice option for people who need some extra help but are not ready for full 24-hour care. Cost for Assisted Living ranges from $1900-$5000 per month and can be paid for with private funds or long-term care insurance. Occasionally in some states Assisted Living Facilities can accept Medicaid.

Nursing Home Care

When independent or assisted living is no longer a viable option, a nursing home will provide 24-hour care by trained and licensed staff. A Registered Nurse or Licensed Practical Nurse is on duty at all times. Some nursing homes are private pay only, some take Medicare, and some will accept Medicaid as payment for services. Most residents live in a semi-private room (private if they can afford it), and are allowed to decorate with their own personal belongings. There are new trends in nursing home care called The Eden Alternative ™. These programs incorporate living things like plants, animals, and children into residential care facilities to make them more like a home, rather than an institution for the frail and elderly. The average cost for a semi-private nursing home bed nationwide in 2007 is around $206.00 per day ($6180 per month) or more.

Tips for Choosing an Assisted Living or Nursing Care Facility

Choosing a facility for a loved one, or even for yourself, can be difficult and time consuming. The following tips and hints will help give you guidance when trying to make that decision. Remember—take notes on each facility you visit and compare them later.

- Speak with people you trust about their experiences with Nursing Homes.
- Pick a good location.
- Ask the home about bed availability.
- Do they have Medicare, Medicaid, or private pay beds available?
- What is the staffing arrangement? RNS? LPNS? CNAS?
- Are there extra services and fees?

- Is the home able to provide for special care needs such as Alzheimer's, End Stage Renal Disease, or other medical conditions?
- *Visit the homes on your list!* Nothing replaces a tour.
- Ask to see a copy of the most recent state inspection. Or visit the Nursing Home Compare site on the web at *www.medicare.gov*.
- Do the residents seem to have a good quality of life?
- How long has the current staff been working at the facility?
- Does the facility conduct background checks for criminal and elder abuse activity prior to hiring employees?
- Upon entering the facility, pay attention to what you *see* and what you *smell*.
- What are the visiting hours?
- Security? Safety plans for fire evacuations etc?
- Be sure to visit the home at least once when they are not expecting you.
- Make an inventory of the items that you or your loved one brings to the home for future reference.
- Talk to some of the other visitors/ family members. How do they feel about the care provided?

PART TWO

Planning Ahead for Long-Term Care— Avoid the Crisis

SENIOR SOLUTION #1

Planning Ahead for Long-Term Care Means Evaluating All the Options

How Much Does Long-Term Care Insurance Cost?

Of course the cost of long-term care insurance depends on many different choices and options. The more bells and whistles you choose, the more costly the plan. The most important thing to remember is that long-term care insurance premiums will NEVER cost as much as a few months in a nursing home without the insurance (see Chapter 1). The problem for most people is that long-term care insurance premiums may seem unaffordable, even though it's the most cost effective way to plan ahead.

Affording Long-Term Care Insurance Without Touching a Penny of Your Savings, Investments, or Current Income

Today many seniors 62 and older who own their own homes are taking advantage of reverse mortgages to pay their long-term care insurance premiums.

Example: Affording Long-Term Care Insurance

Mary and Joe Black live in St. Louis, Missouri and are both 65 years old. They own a home worth $200,000. Both are in good health. They are interested in a 5 year plan, with compound inflation protection, and a 90-day elimination period (waiting period). They chose $150 per day coverage because they have other income and assets to make up for any shortfall. The average cost for a nursing home bed in 2007 is around $207 per day.

The annual premium total for both to have coverage is $5460.

The Blacks are eligible to receive $605 per month for life from the equity in their home (a reverse mortgage), or a lump sum of $99, 657, or any combination of the two.

They can also leave the $99,657 in a line of credit that currently grows at a rate of 6.35% (*Old number from 2006, these rates change weekly!!). This means that if they didn't need the extra cash for any reason, they could take approximately $6328 annually out of their line of credit to pay for their long-term care insurance premium.

Alternatively, they could pay their monthly premium of $455 with the $605 monthly check that they would receive from the reverse mortgage lender.

Either way they have protected themselves from the catastrophic expense of long-term care without touching a penny of their savings, investments, or current income.

The Blacks really wanted to give their children the value of their home as an inheritance. They were concerned that if they took out a reverse mortgage to pay for long-term care insurance, there wouldn't be anything left over to give their children!

So in addition, the Blacks increased the value of their estate for their heirs by purchasing a "2nd to Die" life insurance policy (which pays after both spouses have passed away) for $250,000. This leaves an inheritance of $250,000 for their heirs instead of the $200,000 home value that they

> originally had. Plus that inheritance of $250,000 is all tax free money for their heirs, and avoids PROBATE!

Traditional Long-Term Care Insurance

Traditional Long-Term Care Insurance used to be viewed as "nursing home insurance" because most policies from 15 years ago only offered that one option. Today that is hardly the case. Long-term care insurance now covers adult day care, in-home care, assisted living, and nursing home care. These policies are considered comprehensive in nature. Now we refer to long-term care insurance as "lifestyle insurance".

Who CAN'T Get Long-Term Care Insurance?

Underwriting Explained

When you apply for a Long-Term Care Insurance plan, you must go through underwriting. Underwriting means that the company will check your medical records to determine what medical problems you may currently have, or have had in the past. They want to know your overall health history. If you have been diagnosed with short-term memory loss, Alzheimer's disease, Parkinson's disease, Multiple Sclerosis, Lou Gehrig's disease, or if you have had a stroke with permanent physical impairment, you may not qualify. People who have survived cancer and are treatment free for a certain length of time can often qualify. Each insurance company has their own underwriting guidelines. It is best to talk to your agent or call the company directly with any specific questions about health issues. Height and weight are also a consideration when applying. Sometimes the insurance company will send a registered nurse to the home to ask a few questions, and take some more medical history, or they may just call on the phone for a brief interview.

Qualifying to USE the Benefits of a Long-Term Care Insurance Plan

Activities of Daily Living

When it's time to use your tax qualified Long-Term Care Insurance plan (taxes to be discussed in a later chapter), the insured person must need help or substantial assistance with 2 out of 6 activities of daily living for a period of 90 days or greater. This need for care must be certified by a licensed healthcare practitioner such as a nurse or physician.

These activities of daily living include:

- Bathing
- Dressing
- Eating
- Toileting
- Continence
- Transferring (i.e. moving from the bed to a chair)

Or the insured must have a cognitive impairment like Alzheimer's disease or dementia. A cognitive impairment means that although a person may be physically able to perform all of the activities listed above, they cannot remember or rationalize how to do those activities. One example would be bathing. Sometimes people with dementia are physically able to take a bath, but can't remember to do so, or can't remember why this is important. Or perhaps when getting dressed, they put on 5 shirts instead of one.

Comprehensive vs. Facility Only Plans

Comprehensive Plans

A comprehensive plan covers all aspects of long-term care: in-home care, adult day care, assisted living, and nursing home care. These plans are designed to help people stay at home longer and also assist them with transitions to other levels of care as needed. Most consumers want to stay at home for as long as possible. A comprehensive plan will satisfy that desire.

Facility Only Coverage

Facility only plans are still available on the market today. Facility only plans pay for just that, facility care only. Usually this includes assisted living and nursing home care. A facility only plan makes the most sense for folks who do not have a large network of family and friends around them, and for people who know that this may be their only option in the future. Facility only plans are less costly than comprehensive plans but again, offer payment only for nursing home and assisted living care. The insured person cannot live at home and use the benefits of a facility only plan.

Benefit Period

The benefit period is the length of time the policy will actually pay for care. There are many different benefit periods available including 2 years, 3 years, 4 years, 5 years, 7 years, 10 years, and unlimited lifetime coverage. When purchasing long-term care insurance keep in mind that premiums are paid for potentially the next 20 years (or until the policy holder needs care), but the plan will only last about as long as the benefit period originally selected.

People often ask, "How do I know which benefit period to choose?" "How do I know how long I might need care?"

Obviously there is no way to really determine how long a person might need care. However the best advice is for each individual to take a look at their own personal health history and their family history. If there is a history of chronic disease such as Alzheimer's, Parkinson's, MS, or Lou Gehrig's disease, it might be worthwhile to consider a longer benefit period.

> TIP: The average length of stay in a nursing home is about 2.8 years; the average care giving time at home is about 4.1 years.

Daily Benefit Amount

The daily benefit amount is the maximum amount a plan will pay on a daily or weekly basis. Some policies now pay based on a weekly or monthly maximum. In this case, it is important to know the average cost of care in the local area. In the Midwest for example, the average cost of care for a semi-private nursing home bed is about $135 per day. Therefore the plan should pay a maximum of $4,050 per month. Currently in New York the cost of a semi-private nursing home bed is around $250 per day or $7,500 per month. Consider the cost of care in the area where you live and the cost of care in an area where you might retire, and plan accordingly.

A semi-private room in a nursing home means that two people share a room. A private room in a nursing home means that the room is for one person only. A private room will cost significantly more than a semi-private room. Be sure to factor in the extra cost if a private room is expected.

For some people the insurance policy's daily benefit amount doesn't need to cover the entire cost of care. If there is some Social Security income or pension income that can pick up a portion of the long-term care costs, then perhaps some premium can be saved by having a lower daily benefit amount.

Keep in mind however, that $135/day covers the cost of room and board only in the Midwest, not the added cost of prescription drugs, supplies such as adult incontinence protection, and other necessities. The additional expense of these items can add as much as 20% per day on to the cost of a nursing home bed.

Elimination Period

The elimination period is similar to a deductible or a waiting period. This is the length of time a person must wait before their plan will begin to pay. Elimination periods vary from company to company and plan to plan. The elimination period choices include 0 days, 30 days, 60 days, 90 days, 100 days, and 180 days. Some plans will offer to waive the elimination period for home care under certain circumstances, and some offer riders that will eliminate or decrease waiting periods. Be aware that some elimination periods are based on dates of service. Therefore if only one day of home care is needed per week and the elimination period is 30 days, it could take as much as 30 weeks to satisfy that elimination period. On the other hand, many companies today will allow one day of home care to count as 7 days toward the elimination period. This is a nice strategy and is useful in encouraging people to stay home longer.

> TIP: The shorter the elimination period, the more expensive the premium.

Inflation Protection Options

The average cost of health care rises anywhere from 4%-7% per year. Therefore $135 per day today won't be enough coverage 10 years from now when the cost is actually around $250 per day. So it is important to build in some protection against the cost of inflation.

There are typically three types of inflation protection that are available. One is compound inflation protection which provides an automatic increase in benefits every year (usually at 5%) with no corresponding increase in premium. This is the most expensive inflation protection but well worth the investment. For consumers who buy long-term care insurance at younger ages, for example anyone under age 70, compound inflation protection offers the most complete coverage.

Simple inflation protection is also usually at 5% per year but is not compounded. This inflation protection will grow at a slower rate than compound inflation protection and is often recommended for folks over age 70. There is no corresponding increase in premium.

Finally, there is a future purchase option offered on some plans. This option allows the consumer to decide at a later time whether they would like to buy more daily benefit amount to catch up with the current cost of care. If no extra benefit is purchased, the daily benefit amount remains the same and the premium does not increase. If extra benefit is purchased, the premium increases to the new benefit level. No further underwriting is required for future purchase option benefit increases.

Care Coordination Benefits

Some plans will offer care coordination as a built in benefit. Care coordination is a valuable service for both the person receiving care and for the other family members involved. Long-term care insurers recognize that sometimes it is difficult for a senior or a family member to know which services in their local area might be most appropriate and give the best quality care available. Care coordinators are licensed professionals such as Registered Nurses and Licensed Social Workers who have experience in home health and coordinating care for seniors in their local areas. Some companies will require the plan member to use a care coordinator designated by the insurer. Other companies will allow a family to choose that care coordinator. They will allot a certain amount of money to be used toward a comprehensive in-home evaluation and plan of care. Either way, this service is invaluable and takes the fear and confusion out of selecting a long-term care provider. Care coordinators are not "gatekeepers". They are simply healthcare professionals who know the system and the local resources. They are there for guidance and assistance along the way.

Home Care and Community Care Benefits

Home and Community Care includes services provided by a licensed home health agency. This can include services from a Registered Nurse, Licensed Practical Nurse, Physical Therapist, Occupational Therapist, Nurse's Aide, homemaker services (non-medical services), at-home hospice care, and adult day care. Some plans with enhanced home care provisions, or riders, will also allow (with authorization) a friend or family member to provide care. That family member will be reimbursed for their time and expense. Usually a family member cannot be someone who normally lives in the same home as the person going on claim. In other words, most long-term care insurance companies do not want to pay a spouse to be the sole caregiver.

Facility Care

Facility care most often refers to care received in a Nursing Home, Hospice Facility, or Assisted Living Facility. The plan will usually cover room and board, nursing care, maintenance or personal care, and hospice care in that facility. Most plans will also offer a bed reservation benefit, meaning that if a person leaves the facility for the weekend, or is hospitalized, the insurer will pay for that amount of time to hold the bed even though the insured is not in the facility. Most bed reservation benefits last about 30 days per policy year.

Respite Care Benefits

Respite Care, simply defined, is a break for the caregiver. For example if daughter Susan is caring for her father she may need a break form time to time. If she decides to take a long weekend and go on vacation, a formal caregiver can be hired to take her place. Respite care can be received in a nursing home, adult day care, in-home, or in a hospice facility. The insurer will pay the maximum daily benefit for up to 21 days per year on average. The insured does not have to meet the elimination period in order to use Respite Care benefits.

Alternate Plan of Care

Alternate plan of care usually refers to services that are not already clearly defined in the plan. Most alternate plans of care must be approved by the insurer, but would include services designed to enhance quality of life, or designed to keep a person safe in their home for a longer period of time. Examples include a Personal Emergency Service, like LifeLine, or perhaps a wheelchair ramp that would enhance accessibility to the insured's home.

Caregiver Training

Caregiver Training is useful when an informal caregiver needs to learn how to bathe, transfer, feed, or dress someone receiving long-term care. A licensed or formally trained professional will provide the training to the informal caregiver. This ensures that the care being received is quality care, and is provided in a safe and efficient manner. This training will be paid for by the plan.

Bells and Whistles (The Riders)

Riders can be purchased in addition to the standard long-term care insurance plan and offer flexibility in plan design.

Shared Benefits

Some plans will allow spouses and families to share benefits. One example would be sharing a benefit between husband and wife. In this case, the husband and wife choose an 8-year plan. If he needs to use 6 years of the plan, she will have 2 years left to use when she needs long-term care. A shared benefit plan might be recommended to a couple who have been married for many years and who are roughly the same age.

Survivorship

Survivorship typically means that if both spouses are insured by the same company with no claim having been made in 7-10 years, and one spouse passes away, the other spouse's plan will be paid up in full. There will be no further premium due for the surviving spouse and coverage will continue.

Return of Premium

Return of premium takes away the fear: "If I don't use it, I will lose it!" This simply means that if a claim has never been made and the insured person passes away, the premium paid will be returned to the surviving heirs. There are several variations on the theme and each company handles return of premium differently. Pay close attention to contract language in the policy.

Waiver of Premium

In many cases, waiver of premium is a built in feature of a long-term care insurance plan, but in some cases it can be purchased as an extra rider. Waiver of premium means that when the insured files a claim and begins using their benefits, they no longer pay premiums to the insurance company. Usually, waiver of premium goes into effect after the elimination period has been satisfied.

Indemnity

The typical long-term care insurance plan is a reimbursement plan, meaning that the insurance company reimburses the care providers after a claim has been sent in. However some plans now offer an indemnity situation. This type of plan will pay the insured the daily or monthly benefit, and it is up to the insured to pay the care providers. This type of plan is more flexible and usually more expensive. However the insured has more options when choosing a care provider. For instance, instead of using a local home health agency, the insured person may want to pay a son or daughter to care for them. Indemnity plans require that the insured, or their legal representative, makes good choices about care and is able to use the money wisely.

Important Considerations When Choosing a Long-Term Care Plan

Ratings

Financial ratings of a company are important when considering purchasing a long-term care insurance plan. The recommendation is to choose a company with an AM BEST rating of A+ or better.

Assets

Assets of the insurance company should be in the BILLIONS.

Discounts

Some long-term care insurers will allow for group discounts through employers, or "affinity" group discounts through a local organization. Senior clubs and organizations all across America offer discounts from 5%-10% on long-term care insurance. Not all companies permit these types of discounts however there are some discounts that almost all long-term care insurers include in their plans. Those include spousal (or partner) discounts and good health discounts. Spousal discounts are applied when a couple applies for the insurance together. Discounts of this kind range anywhere from 30-50%. Good health discounts are given when the applicant is in excellent health. Each company has it's own underwriting guidelines for health discounts. These will range from 10%-15%.

Tax Considerations

Currently there are some tax advantages regarding tax qualified long-term care insurance plans. At the Federal level, premiums for long-term care insurance fall into the "medical expense" category. So if the premium (or the premium plus other medical expenses) is over 7.5% of the adjusted gross income, part of that premium is tax deductible. Below is a table that determines how much of the premium is deductible. Tax payers must be able to itemize in order to take advantage of the federal deduction. It is important to talk to a tax advisor or accountant for that information, as it changes every year.

The 2007 deductible limits under Section 213(d)(10) for eligible long-term care premiums includable in the term 'medical care' are as follows:

Attained Age Before Close of Taxable Year & Max. Limit

Age 40 or less – $ 290
More than 40 but not more than 50 – $ 550
More than 50 but not more than 60 – $1,110
More than 60 but not more than 70 – $2,950
More than 70 – $3,680

Source: IRS Revenue Procedure 2006-53 2007 limits

Business owners, especially those with C-Corporations, can deduct the full cost of long-term care insurance protection for themselves and designated individuals, including spouses.

On the state level, 26 states offer some form of deduction or tax credit for long-term care insurance premiums. In the state of Missouri, for example, premiums are 50% tax deductible. This is an "above the line" deduction so there is no need to itemize to take advantage of the savings. In Kentucky the premium is 100% tax deductible. Again it is important to see an accountant or tax advisor for tax advantages state by state.

Tax Qualified Plans vs. Non-Tax Qualified Plans

To make matters a little more complicated, there are two types of standard Long-Term Care Insurance plans available. Tax qualified plans follow the Federal HIPAA law (Health Insurance Portability and Accountability Act). For these plans the insured must need assistance or help with 2 out of 6 activities of daily living, for a period of 90 days or greater, in order to qualify to use their benefits. This law protects consumers in several ways. It insures that long-term care insurance is truly designed for Long-term care… greater than 90 days. The benefits received are not considered taxable income. Tax qualified plans are *guaranteed renewable.* This means that your coverage can never be cancelled, as long as you pay your premiums.

Non-tax qualified plans allow the consumer to access benefits more quickly. With these plans the insured only needs to prove that they require assistance with 1 out of 5 activities of daily living, with an attending physician's statement. Non-tax qualified plans are usually a bit more expensive than tax qualified. The jury is still out on whether or not the benefits are taxable as income. In the insurance world, there is a great debate on the pros and cons of each plan. Sticking with a tax-qualified plan is currently my recommendation.

Payment Options for Long-Term Care Insurance

Annual Premium Payment

Annual premium payment means that the insured person will pay premiums yearly for a lifetime or until they use their long-term care insurance. Payments can also be made monthly, quarterly, or semi-annually. Like auto or homeowners insurance, if payments are made on a monthly, quarterly, or semi-annual basis, there is usually an additional fee. Once the insured has a claim approved most policies will waive the premium after the elimination period has been satisfied.

10-Pay

The 10-pay option allows the insured to pay a higher premium for a shorter period of time- 10 years. After 10 years of premium payment no further premiums are due.

Pay to 65

Some plans offer the option for the insured person to pay premiums until they are 65. At age 65 no further premium is due. This is a nice option because at retirement age, income may be significantly less than for working age adults.

Lump Sum (One Time) Payment

Some consumers have the option to pay a one-time lump-sum premium. This means that no further premium is ever due. Many business owners find this option attractive for the tax deduction in the year that they purchase the policy. Asset based long-term care insurance is also a one time payment.

Paying With Interest from an Annuity

There is a way to pay for long-term care insurance without ever writing a check. Some consumers will assign the interest earned from an annuity to pay their annual premium.

Required Minimum Distribution

At age 70 ? it is time to take the minimum distribution from an IRA or 401K. Some consumers may not need the extra income, and will use their minimum distribution to pay their annual long-term care insurance premium.

SENIOR SOLUTION #1

The Pension Protection Act of 2006

On August 17, 2006 the President signed into law The Pension Protection Act of 2006 (the "Act"). Individuals owning annuity contracts can now have long-term care riders with special tax consequences. The Act allows the cash value of annuity contracts to be used to pay premiums on long-term care contracts. The payment of premiums in this manner will reduce the cost basis of the annuity contract. In addition the Act also allows annuity contracts with long-term care riders to be exchanged for contracts without such a rider in a tax-free transfer under Section 1035 of the Internal Revenue Code of 1986, as amended ("IRC"). This provision may prove beneficial to individuals who own annuities with a large cost basis. The cash value of the annuity can be used to purchase long-term care insurance. This provision is effective for exchanges which take place after 2009.

Asset Based Long-Term Care Insurance

"Legacy Assets" are those assets in a retiree's portfolio that do not support their lifestyle, but are available in case of some serious emergency (rainy day money!). These assets, if (hopefully) never needed, will probably pass to the clients' children, church or charity after they die. The one most significant risk to those assets is the need to pay for long-term care.

Many people in this situation resist the idea of conventional long-term care insurance; not wanting to admit that they might need it, and taking the position that they can pay for any care out of pocket. They are choosing to "self insure". For these individuals, the ideal planning approach would be to "invest" some of their legacy assets in such a way that the assets can be worth as much as possible whenever they may be needed to pay for care… in the home, assisted living facility or nursing home. If not needed the money would then pass to the intended heirs, with no "use it, or lose it" issues as with conventional long-term care insurance.

To employ this strategy money is transferred from its current location (bank account, fixed annuity, etc) into a specially designed life insurance policy with riders that prepay the death benefit, and additionally to reimburse the insured for the incurred costs of long-term care. Depending on age, sex and health status, the money paid into one of these policies may be worth twice as much if the insured dies without ever needing to use it. And if needed for convalescent care, the insured can receive the expanded death benefit—as much as 50% per year can be paid for long-term care. In a generic example, that means a $50,000 deposit into one of these insurance policies would pay $100,000 to reimburse the insured for convalescent care costs. Any money not used for that purpose would then pass to the heirs at death.

While invested in the insurance policy, the client's money is safe and available for any other reason at any time. Usually there is a money-back guarantee that assures the policyholder will always have access to the funds. Rather than a typical "purchase" of insurance, the transaction is more like "moving money from one account to another"…a cash value account that provides the same "savings" features as the bank, bond or annuity from which it came.

Because the actual cost of long-term care is so great (potentially $70,000 per year or more) and the average need exceeds 2 years, these policies are usually purchased with a rider that extends the long-term care benefits after the death benefit has been exhausted. These riders effectively double or triple the benefit so that in the example above, a $50,000 premium deposit can provide as much as $300,000 in total long-term care benefits, providing as much as six years worth of protection.

This approach is ideal for those individuals who reject the idea of purchasing conventional annual premium long-term care insurance policies and take the position that if they ever need long-term convalescent care, they will pay for it using their own assets.

For individuals who do not, for whatever reason, want to own any life insurance, there is an alternative. Since the objective is to leverage up the individual's assets if long-term care is needed, some insurance companies are now offering fixed annuities with long-term care benefits.

SENIOR SOLUTION #1

Unlike life insurance, fixed deferred annuities are simply an alternative "savings account". Money is deposited with the insurance company, earns tax-deferred interest (usually a little higher than that paid by a bank) and is available to the owner at any time as a partial withdrawal, total lump sum liquidation, or guaranteed monthly payments. This annuity however, adds an additional feature that provides reimbursement for long-term care expenses up to 300% of the annuity value. Recently passed legislation designed to encourage people to plan for long-term care now allows the insurance company to distribute the annuity values income-tax free when needed for long-term care.

Finally, of all the contingencies faced in retirement, long-term care is probably the most difficult and perhaps the most costly…financially as well as emotionally. These asset based long-term care strategies allow wise consumers to manage their money, and to provide significantly for such a possibility without committing large annual insurance premiums to something they sincerely hope will never be needed. Since the money to do this must reside somewhere, these asset based long-term care products provide a safe and financially rewarding option.

The information above on asset based long-term care insurance was contributed by Gene Pastula, CFP, of Westland Financial Services Inc., www.westlandinc.com , 888-238-8154

Asset Based Long-Term Care Insurance Example:

- Jane Smith lives in St. Louis, Missouri.
- Jane is a 70 year old non-smoker in good health.
- She owns a home worth $250,000. She owes nothing on her home.
- Jane has approximately $122,000 in equity available to her by using a reverse mortgage.
- She takes $100,000 out of that equity out and purchases a **single–premium asset based Long-Term Care Insurance plan.**

- She now has $412,101 available to pay for long-term care if she needs it ($190/day for 6 years).
- Her death benefit is $137,367 if she never uses her long-term care insurance benefit.
- The original $100,000 premium is available to be transferred back to her at any time if she changes her mind.
- If Jane died at age 86 and never used her long-term care insurance plan, she would have $137,367 to pass on to her heirs, PLUS $154,517 in retained equity in her home, for a total of $291,684 in inheritance.

Life Settlements

Seniors and their family members should know that there is another option for a life insurance policy that is going to lapse or surrender to the insurance company.

This option is called a *life settlement*, also known as a life insurance settlement. A life settlement is a new financial planning tool for seniors who may have a life insurance policy that they no longer need or want. A life settlement is a lump cash payment that is greater than the policy's cash surrender value and less than the death benefit. Never before have non-terminal policyholders been able to receive capital in excess of their policy's cash or surrender value to increase their wealth. A life settlement can usually provide anywhere from 2 to 5 times the cash surrender value of the policy.

Some requirements and conditions must be met for a senior to be able to utilize a life settlement. Please remember that these are general conditions and each case is looked at individually:

- The insured must be at least 65 years of age.
- The insured has experienced a decline in health since the issue date.

SENIOR SOLUTION #1

- The insured's life expectancy is 17 years or less.
- The face amount of the policy is at least $100,000.
- The policy is beyond the two-year contestable period.

The types of insurance policies that qualify for a potential life settlement are:

- term
- whole life
- universal life
- joint-survivorship
- group
- corporate-owned policies (COLI)
- key-man
- life policies held in irrevocable life insurance trusts

Why would anyone want to sell their life insurance policy? Here are some situations in which the policy owner may want to consider a life settlement:

- The policy owner can no longer pay the premiums and needs relief from them. This is a common situation during retirement when income levels have changed and the premium payment can be strain on finances.
- The policy is lapsing or surrendering because it is no longer needed for a variety of circumstances. This is one of the primary reasons to determine if a life settlement is available. If the policy is going to lapse it is wise to explore the option of selling the policy and receiving a lump sum of money.
- New insurance coverage or a financial product better fits your current needs. Cost of insurance has changed considerably in the last few years. It is a good time to evaluate your current insurance needs and see if a better performing and cost efficient product is available.

- The policy owner needs cash now, such as for medical needs, to assist children or grandchildren, or to supplement retirement income.
- The insured has outlived the beneficiaries.
- For estate tax planning purposes, it no longer makes sense for the policy to pay out as planned. An example would be that the estate no longer needs insurance for liquidity.
- A company's key man is retiring, thus ending the need to maintain insurance on his or her life.
- A buy-sell agreement backed by insurance has been completed.

There are numerous situations in which a life settlement can be beneficial. The reality is that thousands of seniors across the nation are lapsing or surrendering their policies without the knowledge that a life settlement could be available. Now, policies that would have been lapsed or forfeited without determining the fair market value can be sold to investment firms and funding sources for true value.

The life settlement process is not complicated at all. The policy owner would first simply fill out a life settlement application and requested authorizations. The application includes authorizations to collect medical records and up to date information about the policy to be sold from the applicant's insurance carrier. *Unlike a life insurance application there is no medical examination or physical required.*

The settlement company then would retrieve the needed information including attending physician statements, and insurance policy for review. This information would then be submitted to several funding organizations to receive the highest possible settlement. Settlement offers are then relayed to the policy owner or their representative for acceptance. Upon acceptance of an offer, contracts and insurance policy change of ownership documents are forwarded to the policy owner or their representative for review and signatures. The signed documents are returned to the funding organization. The documents are then forwarded to the insurance company to record the change of ownership.

SENIOR SOLUTION #1

Upon written verification that changes of ownership and beneficiary have been recorded, settlement funds are paid to the policy owner. At this point the policy owner has 15 days to change their mind and cancel the transaction. The process typically takes 3 to 6 weeks to complete, depending on how long it takes to receive documents such as physician statements.

Another important benefit of the life settlement process is that *there is never a cost or obligation* involved in determining if a life settlement is available to the policy owner. As previously stated, not every individual will qualify for a life settlement and each situation is looked at individually. However, since there is of no cost or obligation there should be no reason not to explore the option of a life settlement.

In summary, a life insurance settlement is a strong and beneficial financial tool for senior policy owners. With this consumer friendly approach, senior policy owners now have options to receive more money, versus the previously limited options of only a cash surrender or policy lapse.

Grant Shellhammer contributed this information and is a Life Settlement Specialist and works with senior clients on a nationwide basis. He can be reached at 1-888-973-8377 or his website at www.LifeSettlementPro.com. He would be glad to assist and answer any questions regarding your life settlement needs.

SENIOR SOLUTION #2

The Best New Way to Consider Your Estate Planning Needs— Using Home Equity to Your Advantage

Passing on the Value of Your Home to Your Heirs

Many seniors could use extra cash flow from a reverse mortgage to pay for long-term care, home maintenance, repairs, to pay off debt and much more. However they prefer to leave an inheritance to their heirs at the time of their death. A number of seniors would like to leave the value of their home to their heirs. What they may not realize is that a home or property not protected by a trust will certainly have to pass through probate court which can be costly and time consuming. Therefore many seniors have instead chosen to purchase life insurance using the equity in their home (a reverse mortgage). Some seniors, if healthy enough, can double or even triple the value of their estates using reverse mortgage proceeds to purchase life insurance.

Passing on an estate using life insurance proceeds means that the inheritance avoids taxes and probate.

> ### Home Equity Estate Planning Example:
>
> Betty Jones lives in Kansas City, Missouri. She has decided to purchase long-term care insurance and life insurance. Without the help of a reverse mortgage Betty would not be able to afford these premiums without changing her lifestyle dramatically. By using the equity in her home she will protect herself against the catastrophic cost of long-term care and she will also pass on more than the value of her home to her heirs.
>
> - Betty is 65 years old, and in good health. She is a non-smoker.
> - Betty owns a home worth $200,000. There is no debt against the home.
> - Betty buys a 5 year long-term care insurance plan.
> - Compound inflation protection is included.
> - She has a 90–day elimination period (waiting period).
> - The plan pays $150/day for comprehensive care.
> - Annual premium total for her to have this long-term care coverage: $4548
> - Betty is eligible to receive a lump sum of $99,657 from the equity in her home.
> - She will purchase a life insurance policy by paying a one time premium of $50,000.
> - Betty leaves the remaining $49,657 in a line of credit that grows at *6.35% per year (2006 interest rates- note these change weekly). She pays her annual long-term care insurance premium from the line of credit every year.
> - This means that Betty will leave her heirs a death benefit of $222,736 plus the value of her home minus her loan balance.

SENIOR SOLUTION #2

She will be protected from the catastrophic cost of long-term care, and will be able to stay in her home to receive that care.

- She has now helped her heirs to receive a tax free inheritance that is worth more than the current value of her home.

Betty did all of this without touching a penny of her savings, investments, or current income. In fact, now she and her heirs have the cash flow they needed to keep her safe for her remaining years.

Conclusion

It comes as no surprise to anyone that the family dynamic in America has changed over the years. Seniors often worry about outliving their money and what would happen if they ever really did need expensive long-term care!? Economics demand that most of us of "working age" have two-income families, and we find ourselves busy with our children's extra-curricular activities. Furthermore, most of us with aging family members have had that thought in the back of our minds more than once- "What are we going to do with/for Mom and Dad when the time comes where they can no longer care for themselves?"

Most seniors today live independently or at home with some form of assistance coming in to attend to their needs. Only 20% of seniors who need care are actually in nursing homes, while 80% are cared for in a home-like setting.

Every stage of our lives brings with it changes, fears, obstacles, questions, wonders, opportunities, happy times, and not-so-happy times. Seniors will tell you that their greatest fears are losing their autonomy, dignity, respect, and independence. Above all else they are afraid of outliving their money and being put in a nursing home for their remaining days.

Everyone wants to live at home for life. I have yet to meet an aging adult who will tell you that they ultimately prefer to live in a nursing home. For some the process is inevitable. There may come a time for many of us when care at home becomes impossible, mainly for safety or economic reasons.

Although in-home care is less costly than nursing home care, 24/7 in-home care is difficult for most families to afford to pay for privately. Long-term care insurance is one solution to keeping seniors safe and at home for longer periods of time. Planning ahead for long-term care has never been a more important concept. However for some seniors and their families, it's either too late (poor health), or too expensive to afford long-term care insurance.

There are other solutions and ways to manage the crisis of long-term care needs for seniors. There are ways that seniors can help themselves, and families can rest easier knowing that Mom and Dad will be taken care of with the dignity and respect they deserve. All of this can now happen *at home* for much longer periods of time. Education empowers consumers to remain independent for as long as possible. Talk with each other about long-term care issues and concerns in your family before crisis happens.

The Senior Solution Rolodex

The following listings are resources available to seniors and their family members nationwide.

Financial Planning Assistance

Next Generation Financial Services
a division of 1st Mariner Bank

Financial Advisors and Agents located nationwide offering a variety of services including reverse mortgages, long-term care insurance, life insurance, life settlements, annuities and other financial planning strategies.

(877) 203-5667

www.reversemortgagenation.org

The Financial Planning Association—FPA
5775 Glenridge Drive, NE
Suite B-300
Atlanta, GA 30328
www.fpanet.org

National Association of Personal Financial Advisors—NAPFA
355 W. Dundee Rd. Suite 200
Buffalo Grove, IL 60089
(888) FEE-ONLY
www.napfa.org

Reverse Mortgage Information and Services

Next Generation Financial Services
a division of 1st Mariner Bank

Financial Advisors and Agents located nationwide offering a variety of services including reverse mortgages, long-term care insurance, life insurance, life settlements, annuities and other financial planning strategies.
(877) 203-5667
www.reversemortgagenation.org

National Reverse Mortgage Lenders Association
1400 16th St., NW
Suite 420
Washington, DC 20036
(202) 939-1760
www.nrmla.org

Life Settlements

Life Settlement Pro
202 Lonesome Pine Dr.
Longwood, FL 32779
Toll Free: (888) 973-8377 eFax: (206) 333-0112
www.lifesettlementpro.com

Long-Term Care Insurance/Health Insurance

Weiss Ratings, Inc.
4176 Burns Road
Palm Beach Gardens, FL 33410
(800) 289-9222
www.weissratings.com

Financial ratings on Long-Term Care Insurance companies can be found here.

National Association of Insurance Commissioners—NAIC
Hall of States
444 North Capitol Street, NW
Suite 701
Washington, DC 20001-1512
(202) 624-7790
www.naic.org

Health Insurance Association of America, Public Affairs Department—HIAA
555 13th St., NW
Suite 600
Washington, DC 20004
(202) 824-1600
www.hiaa.org

American Association of Long-Term Care Insurance
AALTCI
3835 E. Thousand Oaks Blvd. Suite 336
Westlake Village, CA 91362
(818) 597-3227
www.aaltci.org

Long-Term Care Insurance Educational Foundation
P.O. Box 370
Centerville, VA 20122
www.ltcedfoundation.org

The Center for Long-Term Care Reform
2212 Queen Anne Ave North #110
Seattle, WA 98109
(206) 283-7036
www.centerltc.org

Government Agencies of Interest

Department of Veterans Affairs (VA)
810 Vermont Ave. NW
Washington, DC 20420
(800) 827-1000
www.va.gov

Paralyzed Veterans of America (PVA)
Veterans Benefits Dept.
801 18th St., NW
Washington, DC 20006
(800) 424-8200
www.pva.org

Centers for Medicare & Medicaid Services (CMS)
Region VII
Richard Bolling Federal Building
Room 235
601 East 12th Street
Kansas City, Missouri 64106
(800) MEDICARE
www.medicare.gov

THE SENIOR SOLUTION ROLODEX

Centers for Medicare and Medicaid Services (CMS), formerly the Health Care Financing Administration—CMS

200 Independence Avenue, SW
Room 303-D
Washington, DC 20201
(877) 267-2323
question@cms.gov
www.cms.gov

"As of July 1, 2001, the Health Care Financing Administration (HCFA) is now the Centers for Medicare & Medicaid Services (CMS). It's more than just a new name—it's an increased emphasis on responsiveness to beneficiaries and providers, and quality improvement."—cms.gov

Area Agencies on Aging

Eldercare Locator
927 15th St. NW, 6th Floor
Washington, DC 20005
Eldercare Locator: (800) 677-1116
www.n4a.org
www.eldercare.gov

First Gov for Seniors

www.seniors.gov

National Institute on Aging

www.nih.gov/nia

National Council on Aging

1901 L Street, N.W.
4th floor
Washington, D.C. 20036
Phone: (202) 479-1200
TDD: (202) 479-6674
info@ncoa.org
www.ncoa.org

Legal Resources

Commission on Legal Problems of the Elderly
www.abanet.org/elderly

National Academy of Elder Law Attorneys
1604 N Country Club Road
Tucson, AZ 85716
www.naela.org

SeniorLaw
www.seniorlaw.com

Caregiver Resources:
Home Care and Adult Day Care

National Adult Day Services Association, Inc.
8201 Greensboro Drive, Suite 300
McLean, Virginia 22102
Toll Free Phone: (866) 890-7357 or (703) 610-9035
info@nadsa.org
www.nadsa.org

National Association for Home Care
228 7th Street, SE
Washington, DC 20003
(202) 547-7424
www.nahc.org

ABLEDATA—Assistive Devices
8630 Fenton Street, Suite 930
Silver Spring, MD 20910
Phone: (800) 227-0216
TTY: (301) 608-8912
www.abledata.com

Meals on Wheels Association of America
www.mowaa.org

Caregiver Resources: Hospice

Partnership For Caring
1620 Eye Street NW, Suite 202,
Washington, DC 20006
Phone: 202-296-8071
Hotline: 800-989-9455
www.caringinfo.org

Hospice Foundation of America
2001 S St. NW #300
Washington DC 20009
Phone: 800-854-3402
www.hospicefoundation.org

National Hospice & Palliative Care Organization (NHPCO)
1700 Diagonal Road, Suite 625
Alexandria, Virginia 22314
Phone: (703) 837-1500
The NHPCO Helpline: (800) 658-8898
www.nhpco.org

Resources for Caregivers: Housing

The Assisted Living Federation of America
11200 Waples Mill Rd
Suite 150
Fairfax, VA 22030
Phone: (703) 691-8100
info@alfa.org
www.alfa.org

National Shared Housing Resource Center
www.nationalsharedhousing.org

National Center for Assisted Living—NCAL
1201 L Street, NW
Washington, DC 20005
Phone: (202) 842-4444
www.ncal.org

American Association of Homes and Services for the Aging—AAHSA
2519 Connecticut Ave. NW
Washington, DC 20008
Phone: 800-508-9442
www.aahsa.org

The Eden Alternative (tm)
www.edenalt.com

Caregiver Resources: Geriatric Care Management

National Association of Professional Geriatric Care Managers
1604 N Country Club Road
Tucson, AZ 85716
www.caremanager.org

Mid West Chapter—Nat'l Assoc. of Professional Geriatric Care Managers
www.midwestgcm.org

The LTC Expert
www.theltcexpert.com
www.seniorslivebetter.com
www.aginganswer.com
www.4seniorsathome.com

Caregiver Resources: Medications

American Pharmaceutical Association—APhA
2215 Constitution Avenue, NW
Washington, DC 20037-2985
800-237-APHA
mail@aphanet.org
www.aphanet.org

Center Watch—Clinical Drug Trials Listings
www.centerwatch.com

MEDLINEplus
www.nlm.nih.gov/medlineplus

Caregiver Resources: Finding Doctors

American Medical Association—AMA
515 North State Street
Chicago, IL 60610
Phone: (312) 464-4818
amalibrary@ama-assn.org
www.ama-assn.org

Gerontological Society of America
www.geron.org

Caregiver Resources: Caregiver Organizations and Support

Children of Aging Parents
1609 Woodbourne Road, Suite 302A
Levittown, PA 19057 USA
Phone: (800) 277-7294
www.caps4caregivers.org

National Family Caregivers Association
10400 Connecticut Avenue, #500
Kensington, MD 20895-3944
(800) 896-3650
www.nfcacares.org

Saint Clare's Health Services (Self Help Groups)
25 Pocono Road
Denville, NJ 07834-2995
Phone: (973) 326-6789
www.selfhelpgroups.org

THE SENIOR SOLUTION ROLODEX

The Well Spouse Foundation
63 West Main Street, Suite H
Freehold, NJ 07728
Phone: (800) 838-0879
www.wellspouse.org

Other Caregiver Sites of Interest
www.caregiving.com
www.caregiver.com
www.carescout.com
http://griefnet.org

Senior Advocacy and Interest Groups

National Consumers League
1701 K Street, NW, Suite 1200
Washington, DC 20006
Phone: (202) 835-3323
www.natlconsumersleague.org

Families USA
www.familiesusa.org

ElderWeb
www.elderweb.com

United Seniors Health Council—USHC
409 3rd St., SW, Suite 200
Washington, DC 20024
Phone: (202) 479-6673
www.unitedseniorshealth.org

American Health Care Association
1201 L Street, N.W.
Washington, DC 20005
Phone: (202) 842-4444
www.ahca.org

Alliance for Retired Americans
888 16th St., N.W.
Suite 520
Washington, D.C. 20006
Phone: (888) 373-6497
www.retiredamericans.org

American Society on Aging—ASA
833 Market Street
Suite 511
San Francisco, CA 94103
(415) 974-9600
info@asaging.org
www.asaging.org

Alliance for Aging Research
2021 K Street, NW
Suite 305
Washington, DC 20006
Phone: (800) 639-2421
info@agingresearch.org
www.agingresearch.org

AARP
www.aarp.org

Benefits Check-Up
www.benefitscheckup.org

Miscellaneous Sites of Interest

Mayo Clinic
www.mayohealth.org

On Health
www.webmd.com

Specific Disease Processes and Organizations On-Line

National Alzheimer's Association
www.alz.org

Alzheimer's Research Forum
www.alzforum.org

Alzheimer's Disease Education and Referral
www.alzheimers.org

American Cancer Society
www.cancer.org

American Diabetes Association
www.diabetes.org

American Heart Association
www.americanheart.org

American Stroke Association
A Division of American Heart Association
7272 Greenville Avenue
Dallas, TX 75231
(888) 4STROKE

strokeassociation@heart.org
www.strokeassociation.org

Arthritis Foundation
www.arthritis.org

National Organization for Rare Disorders
www.rarediseases.org

National Association for Continence
www.nafc.org

National Osteoporosis Foundation
www.nof.org

National Sleep Foundation
www.sleepfoundation.org

Parkinson's Resource Organization
www.parkinsonsresource.org

Self Help for Hard of Hearing People
www.shhh.org

Lighthouse National Center for Vision and Aging—NCVA
111 East 59th Street
New York, NY 10022
(800) 829-0500 (Voice: Toll-free,
Information and Resource Serv.)
(212) 821-9713 (Voice: TDD)
info@lighthouse.org
www.lighthouse.org

About the Author

As seen on NBC's Today Show and CNNFN's "Your Money with Ali Veshi, speaker and author Valerie VanBooven RN, BSN, PGCM is one of the nation's leading long-term care experts and a consultant for consumers and professionals.

Planning ahead for long-term care needs is more important than ever. However many families find themselves in the midst of crisis with an aging family member and need immediate assistance and answers to all of their questions. Valerie addresses both of those issues through her speaking engagements and through her books "Aging Answers" and now "The Senior Solution".

Valerie VanBooven is a *registered nurse, author, professional speaker, and professional geriatric care manager, reverse mortgage expert, as well as a licensed Life and Health Agent in Missouri.*

She currently serves as the National Marketing Director for Next Generation Financial Services, a division of 1st Mariner Bank, headquartered in Baltimore, MD.

After several years of discharge planning and case management for the Unity Health System in St. Louis, Valerie incorporated her own business.

In 1999, *Senior Care Solutions, Inc.* was formed. Valerie is a dedicated Geriatric Care Manager and Long-Term Care Expert.

"I have seen so many families struggle to pay for long-term care costs out of pocket. This can be a devastating situation for everyone involved. My goal is to provide education regarding Long-Term Care Insurance and to help families protect what they have worked so hard to accumulate. I have seen many other families use their Long-Term Care Insurance benefits when they needed them and the bottom line is, it works!"

Valerie is the author of *Aging Answers: Secrets to Successful Long-Term Care Planning, Caregiving, and Crisis Management*, published in 2004, *"Long-Term Care Planning for Insurance Professionals"* published in May 2002 (National Business Institute), and *"Nursing Home Malpractice: From Investigation to Trial"*, April 2003 (National Business Institute).

Mid 2002, Valerie was selected by Phyllis Shelton (President of LTC Consultants, Nashville, TN) as one of 16 presenters to embark on a nationwide tour providing educational seminars for Federal Employees on the new Federal Long-Term Care Insurance Program. Valerie was a regular visitor to the State Department, various bases and forts throughout the country, and various Federal Buildings. She had presented to thousands of attendees.

Valerie is a regular guest speaker for many organizations and groups throughout the country, speaking on various topics related to the aging process, caregiving, long-term care issues, marketing to seniors and baby boomers, and long-term care insurance. She is a member of the National Speakers Association, The National Association of Professional Geriatric Care Managers and Midwest Geriatric Care Managers. She has been a featured guest on various talk radio programs across the country, and hosted her own show called "Healthy Wealthy and Wise" for many years.

Valerie's websites include:

www.theltcexpert.com
www.aginganswer.com
www.seniorslivebetter.com

Valerie's email address:

Valerie@theltcexpert.com